_____

To

_____

From

_____

Date

God's Blessing

Blessing
Day by Day

MyDaily®
Devotional
for Kids

Tommy NELSON®

A Division of Thomas Nelson Publishers
Since 1798

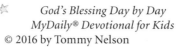

God's Blessing Day by Day
MyDaily® Devotional for Kids
© 2016 by Tommy Nelson

Published in Nashville, Tennessee, by Tommy Nelson. Tommy Nelson is an imprint of Thomas Nelson. Thomas Nelson is a registered trademark of HarperCollins Christian Publishing, Inc.

Tommy Nelson titles may be purchased in bulk for educational, business, fund-raising, or sales promotional use. For information, please e-mail SpecialMarkets@ ThomasNelson.com.

Unless otherwise noted, Scripture quotations are taken from the International Children's Bible®. Copyright © 1986, 1988, 1999, 2015 by Thomas Nelson. Used by permission. All rights reserved.

Scripture quotations marked CEV are taken from the Contemporary English Version. Copyright © 1991, 1992, 1995 by American Bible Society. Used by permission.

Scripture quotations marked NCV are taken from the New Century Version®. © 2005 by Thomas Nelson. Used by permission. All rights reserved.

Scripture quotations marked NIV are taken from the Holy Bible, New International Version®, NIV®. Copyright © 1973, 1978, 1984, 2011 by Biblica, Inc.® Used by permission of Zondervan. All rights reserved worldwide. www. zondervan.com. The "NIV" and "New International Version" are trademarks registered in the United States Patent and Trademark Office by Biblica, Inc.®

Cover and interior design by Kristy L. Edwards
Images copyright Dobrynina Elena / Shutterstock (www.shutterstock.com)

ISBN-13: 978-1-4003-1130-9

Library of Congress Control Number: 2016940163

Printed in China

18 19 20 21 22 DSC 5 4 3 2 1

www.thomasnelson.com

Dear Parents,

Our lives can be very busy. Finding a quiet moment alone with God and His Word can be difficult. This 52-week devotional will help you enjoy those quiet times with your children as you teach them about the Lord and His blessings.

Each day contains a verse, a devotion, a prayer, and a truth about God for your child to remember. Using simple language and charming illustrations, this collection offers messages about telling the truth, doing the right thing (even when no one is looking), and so much more.

Find time each day to spend sharing reminders of God's love and care into your child's heart.

Johnny M. Hunt

Dr. Johnny Hunt
Senior Pastor
First Baptist Church Woodstock
Woodstock, Georgia

Contents

Making God Happy

We have peace with God through our Lord Jesus Christ.
—ROMANS 5:1

I'm guessing you don't like it when you make someone unhappy because of what you did or said. I don't either.

When we do wrong things—when we disobey or are unkind—we make God unhappy. He never does wrong things, and we do wrong things all the time!

That's why God let Jesus come to earth and die on the cross. Jesus was punished for the wrong things you and I do so that God will not be unhappy with us.

Jesus, thank You for helping me to understand when I do things wrong so I can correct my behavior and make God happy with me.

I want to make God happy!

You Are God's Child

If we are God's children, then we will receive the blessings God has for us.

—ROMANS 8:17

T hink about all the good things your mommy and daddy give you!

They make sure you have food and clothes and lots of hugs. They read books and play with you. They might even take you to church and pray with you. Those good things are called blessings!

God is your Daddy in heaven, and He gives you good things too. He loves to share His love and His joy and His beautiful world.

It is good to have God as your Daddy in heaven!

Thank You for being my Daddy in heaven and giving me so many good things.

My Daddy in heaven loves me!

Dr. Johnny Hunt,
First Baptist Church Woodstock, Woodstock, GA

God Does What He Says He'll Do

You get all of God's blessings because of the promise that God made to Abraham.
—GALATIANS 3:29

Do you know what a promise is? It's when you say you will do something.

God is really good at keeping His promises. That means He always does what He says He will do. He always, always, always keeps His promises—and His promises are amazing!

God promises to protect you, give you what you need, comfort you when you're sad, and save a place in heaven for you. God also promises to always be with you, forgive you, and love you—and He will!

Dear God, thank You that You always do what You say You will do!

God is the best Promise Keeper!

4

Dr. Johnny Hunt,
First Baptist Church Woodstock, Woodstock, GA

Being God's Friend

Jesus died so that we could have the Spirit that God promised.
—Galatians 3:14

We can't have dessert if we don't finish our dinner. We can't stay up late when we have school tomorrow.

And we can't know the Holy Spirit until we know Jesus.

If you know that Jesus loves you—and He loves you a lot!—you can know the Holy Spirit. And it is good to know the Holy Spirit because He helps us understand the Bible, He prays for us, He helps us know what God wants us to do, and He helps us do what God wants us to do!

Thank You, Holy Spirit, for praying for me and helping me in so many ways!

I am glad I know the Holy Spirit!

The Best Gift Ever!

The non-Jews will receive what God has for his people.
—Ephesians 3:6

When it's your birthday, maybe you take cupcakes to Sunday school for your class. Those cupcakes are for people in your class and no one else.

But if the kids in your class don't like cupcakes, you can give them to other people at Sunday school.

It's sad, but when God gave the gift of Jesus to His people (called the Jews), not all of them liked Him. So God shared Jesus with other people (the non-Jews). They liked Jesus a lot, so now they are part of God's family.

When you love Jesus, you are part of God's family too!

Dear Lord, thank You for the wonderful gift of Jesus!

Jesus is God's gift to me.

Showing God You Love Him

[God] will not forget the work you did and the love you showed for him by helping his people.
—HEBREWS 6:10

One of the best ways to show God that you love Him is by showing and sharing His love with others. He loves it when you help other people who love Him too.

Did you know that you can show God that you love Him by helping people? There are lots of ways to help people.

At home you can help set the table. At school you can help the teacher clean up. When you're at the store with your mom, you can smile at the cashier.

God always remembers when you help people, and it makes Him smile.

Dear Jesus, I want to show You how much I love You by helping people.

God is happy when I help people.

Dr. Johnny Hunt,
First Baptist Church Woodstock, Woodstock, GA

You're a Gift

Children are a gift from the Lord.

—PSALM 127:3

What was the best gift your dad ever got? Golf clubs? The tie you chose? The picture you drew for him?

What's the best gift your mom ever got? Her new Bible? The pretty necklace?

All those gifts are very special! But the best gift your mom and dad ever got is you! The Bible says, "Children are a gift from the Lord." And a gift that God gives is going to be the *best* kind of gift because He's God!

One way God showed your mom and dad that He loves them was by giving them you!

Lord, thank You for giving me to my mom and dad! I love them!

I am God's gift
to Dad and Mom!

Rev. Nicholas Garner, First Baptist Church, Creedmoor, NC

Love God by Obeying Him

Love the Lord your God. Obey him.
—DEUTERONOMY 30:20

P lease put your toys away!"
"Brush your teeth before church."
Whenever your parents ask you to do something, they want you to listen and do what they say.

God is your Father in heaven, and He wants you and me to listen to what He says and then do what He says. He wants us to listen and obey.

One way we listen to God is to read the Bible and learn that He wants us to love Him and to love other people. Whenever we obey God, we show God that we love Him!

God, please help me show You that I love You by obeying You and my parents.

I show that I love
God by obeying.

It's Good to Give!

Good people always lend freely to others.
—PSALM 37:26

God gives us food, clothes, a home, and everything else we need. Did you know He wants us to share what He gives us with other people?

God wants us to use the blessings He gives us to help give food to people who are hungry and offer clothes to people who don't have enough. When we share with people, they can learn that God loves them.

That's one reason why giving to people who are in need is a good thing to do!

You have given me a lot. Thank You, God! Now please help me share a lot!

When I share, I show God's love.

Telling the Truth

The good person who lives an honest life is a
blessing to his children.

—PROVERBS 20:7

W e don't have to wonder or guess how God wants us to behave. He tells us in the Bible. One thing He tells us is to be completely truthful.

Being truthful means you don't tell your dad that you cleaned your room when it's still messy. Being truthful also means—when your mom asks—you don't say you brushed your teeth when you didn't.

God wants us to tell the truth, and He will help us tell the truth. The Bible says that when we are honest, we will be a blessing to others. And when we tell the truth, we are obeying God and showing Him that we love Him.

God, please help me always tell the truth.

God can help me
always be truthful.

We Have a Helper

"I will put my Spirit into your children. My blessing will be like a stream of water flowing over your family."

—ISAIAH 44:3

I t's hard when someone asks us to do something that we can't do by ourselves. Maybe we're not strong enough or tall enough yet, and we need help.

We all need help being the kind of people God wants us to be. That's why God has given us the Holy Spirit.

The Holy Spirit helps us love people and forgive them. The Holy Spirit can help you obey your parents, be nice to your brother, and share with your sister.

God gave us a big blessing when He gave us the Holy Spirit to help us!

Thank You, God, for giving me the Holy Spirit to help me!

The Holy Spirit is my Helper!

Rev. Nicholas Garner, First Baptist Church, Creedmoor, NC

Real Hope

We hope for the blessings God has for his children. These blessings are kept for you in heaven.

—1 PETER 1:4

Hope means that you look forward to something that God said will happen, knowing that it will definitely happen.

When you hope that God will always love you, that He will always forgive you, and that you'll be able to live in heaven with Him, you can know for sure that those things will happen because God promised them. And that is great news!

God will always love you, He will always forgive you, and He has a place for you in heaven. You can be absolutely sure of getting these blessings, and that's real hope!

God, thank You for the blessings You have for me!

God does what He says He will do.

A Smile Inside

You must completely obey the Lord your God.... Then all these blessings will come and stay with you.
—DEUTERONOMY 28:1-2

T hink about how good it feels when you do something nice. When your mom and dad thank you for helping clear the table or wash the car, you smile inside, don't you?

Doing what God wants you to do can also make you smile inside. God created us to feel good when we do what is right, and it's always right to obey God.

God wants us to tell the truth, worship only Jesus, and treat people the way we want them to treat us. When we obey God and do these things, we smile inside. And that's a blessing!

Please help me obey You, God. I know that obeying You will make me smile inside!

It is always right to obey God!

Doing What's Right

People who do what is right will have rich blessings.

—PROVERBS 10:6

What choices will you make today? Maybe you'll choose what you wear or what friend to play with. You'll also get to choose whether or not to obey your mom, dad, and God.

It's not always easy to make good choices. The Bible tells us about people who made bad choices and people who made good ones. When you and I make bad choices like some people in the Bible did, we make God sad. When we make good choices, we make God happy, and we feel happy. God blesses us when we do what is right.

Thank You, God, for blessing me when I choose to obey You. Please help me to always do what is right.

God is happy when I obey!

Janet Allen Hunt,
First Baptist Church Woodstock, Woodstock, GA

A Happy Heart

A truthful man will have many blessings.
—PROVERBS 28:20

When you have said something that is not true, you probably felt very sad in your heart. Jesus wants us to tell the truth all the time, but when we don't, our hearts become sad. God made us that way. He wants us to feel sad when we don't tell the truth. The sadness reminds us we need to tell the truth.

And the Bible reminds us that God will bless the truthful person. When you tell the truth, you will be full of joy because you will know that you are making God happy.

Jesus, I want to always have a happy heart and be truthful. Thank You for helping me!

Telling the truth makes God happy.

Janet Allen Hunt,
First Baptist Church Woodstock, Woodstock, GA

Listen to God

"Come to me and listen."

—ISAIAH 55:3

Did you hear the special invitation found in the Bible? "Come to Me and listen." That's God talking to you, and He wants *you* to get close to Him and listen to Him.

Reading the Bible is a really good way to get close to God. You'll learn what He wants you to do and that He loves you very, very much.

You'll also learn what He wants you to do to make Him happy. When we listen to and obey God, we show Him that we love Him.

Jesus, please help me understand the Bible and do what the Bible tells me to do.

I can read the Bible and know more about God!

Jesus Loves Us All

The same Lord is the Lord of all and gives many blessings to all who trust in him.

—ROMANS 10:12

When God made people, He made all of us different. There is only one you! And there are a lot of people who are different from you.

God made children with different colored eyes and hair and skin. God gave them different languages to speak, different places to live, different kinds of food to eat, and different kinds of clothes to wear. There are a lot of children in the world, but Jesus loves all of them just the way He loves you—and He loves you a lot!

Jesus, You love all the kids in the world! Thanks for loving me!

Jesus loves kids!
Jesus loves me!

Giving Is Good

God loves the person who gives happily.
—2 CORINTHIANS 9:7

G iving to others is a good thing. It is good to give what God gives us to people who need food, clothes, a house to live in, a Bible to read, and doctors to help them get better.

God wants us to help people by giving them what they need—or money so they can buy what they need—and He wants us to be happy when we give. When it's hard for us to give something away, God will help us give with a happy heart if we ask Him.

God wants us to give to others with a happy face and a happy heart.

Jesus, please help me give with a happy face and a happy heart.

Jesus is happy
when I give.

Janet Allen Hunt,
First Baptist Church Woodstock, Woodstock, GA

I Can Know God!

In Christ, God has given us every spiritual blessing in heaven.

—EPHESIANS 1:3

Ben loved spending time with his grandpa. They went fishing, read stories, or played hide-and-seek. But Ben's *very* favorite thing was sharing an afternoon snack with Grandpa. They would get two cups and fill them with cold milk, and then ... grab the Oreos!

Grandpa let Ben dunk his cookies, and Grandpa didn't care if milk spilled on the table or how messy Ben was. Grandpa loved just being with Ben.

Ben knew his grandpa loved him very much. And Ben also knew—just like you can—that God loves him very much. God's love is a huge blessing!

Thank You, God, for loving me and wanting to spend time with me.

Knowing God is the best thing ever!

Debbie Schreve, First Baptist Church, Texarkana, TX

Be Kind and Helpful

Serving God brings you blessings in this life.
—1 TIMOTHY 4:8

Sarah leaped out of bed. Not only was it Saturday morning. It was Sarah's *favorite* Saturday of the month.

Today she and her family were going to visit some older people who lived near them. And—this was exciting—Sarah got to take her dog, Buddy.

The older people loved to pet Buddy and talk with Sarah. Sometimes Sarah told them a funny story, and other times she sang them a song. Sarah never left without giving each of them a hug, telling them Jesus loves them, and letting them feel Buddy's silky, soft fur.

God, I want to be kind and helpful just like Jesus was.

God is happy when I am kind to others.

A Promise Is a Promise!

Those who are called by God can now receive the blessings that God has promised. These blessings will last forever.
—HEBREWS 9:15

It was report card day. Nick had done his best on his schoolwork, obeyed his teacher, and been nice to all of his classmates.

Nick's mom had promised him a treat if his report card was good. Nick got in the car, handed her his report card, and saw her smile *really* big as she looked at his good grades and the note from his teacher that said Nick was well behaved.

Nick's mom drove him straight to the toy store, just as she promised, and Nick got the toy he had been wanting. God keeps all of His promises too.

You always do what You promise, God! Thank You!

I can depend on God to keep His promises.

God Always Gives Us What We Need

Jesus has the power of God. His power has given us everything we need to live and to serve God.
—2 PETER 1:3

L uke was so surprised! His teacher had given him a special assignment. He had to make his favorite cookies to share with the class the next day.

Luke loved to eat homemade cookies, but he didn't know how to make them. What was he going to do? When he told his mom about it, she said that she had all the ingredients he needed and that she would help him. Together they made the most delicious chocolate chip M&M cookies.

Luke was so thankful for his mom's help. He couldn't have done it without her!

Thank You, God, that You will always help me and always give me what I need.

God gives me everything I need.

The Perfect Gift

Every perfect gift is from God.

—JAMES 1:17

K athryn couldn't wait to save enough allowance money to buy the purple bike of her dreams. But the morning of her birthday, guess what was in the kitchen with a huge bow on it? The purple bike! Her parents had surprised her with a wonderful gift!

"Remember, Kathryn," said Mom, "that everything good is from God. We were able to buy you this bike because He is good to us."

Do you know that the most perfect gift of all is Jesus? God gave Jesus to us, and we should thank Him for such a wonderful gift.

God, thank You for Jesus and for every gift You give.

Everything I have is a gift from God.

Debbie Schreve, First Baptist Church, Texarkana, TX

Use Your Skills

Each of you has received a gift to use to serve others.
Be good servants of God's various gifts of grace.
—1 PETER 4:10 NCV

Steven and Jack were great soccer players. Jill was a great artist. And Ben was pretty great at . . . doing yo-yo tricks!

One day Ben had an idea. He wanted to use his yo-yo tricks to make people smile. So Ben asked his dad, who was a doctor, to see if Ben could visit sick kids in the hospital and show them some tricks. The other doctors liked the idea, and when Ben visited, the kids loved it! They were amazed at Ben's talent. Talking with Ben and watching him do tricks made them feel so much better.

Thank You for giving me skills, God. Help me always use them to make people happy.

I want to help people.

When You Feel Scared

"I am with you, and I will protect you everywhere you go."
—GENESIS 28:15

D id you know that even grown-ups can feel scared sometimes?

One good thing for grown-ups and children to do when they're afraid is to remember that Jesus loves them and that He will always take good care of them.

And when we are afraid, we can always pray: "Dear Jesus, I'm afraid, but I know You love me and will take care of me."

Jesus does love you very much. And He has promised you that He will always take care of you. Remember to thank Jesus for loving you and always being your strong Helper.

Jesus, thank You for always taking care of me, especially when I am afraid.

When I am afraid, I will remember that Jesus loves me.

Jesus—Man with the Plan

All the days planned for me were written in your book before I was one day old.

—PSALM 139:16

Are you ready to hear a very big idea? Here it is! Jesus loves you, and He has loved you since before you were even one day old. Jesus has loved you since before you were born.

And because Jesus loves you, He has good plans for what will happen in your life. Guess what? He made those plans for you before you were born. That is amazing!

But now you *are* born! So remember that Jesus will always love you and always wants good things to happen for you. Jesus has a great plan for your life, and you can trust in His plan.

I am so glad You love me, Jesus! Thank You for making good plans for my life.

> Jesus loves me a lot, and He has great plans for my life.

Just Because You're You!

Jesus said, "Let the little children come to me.
Don't stop them."

—MATTHEW 19:14

O ne time when Jesus was healing people and teaching, some parents and their kids walked toward Him. Jesus' friends wanted to keep the children away. After all, Jesus was very busy. But Jesus wanted the children near Him. Jesus wanted to be their friend because He loves kids!

And Jesus loves *you*! He loves you when you are sad or lonely. He loves you when you drop the ball in centerfield or stumble during the dance recital. He loves you when you are frustrated and angry, laughing and giggling, playing and praying.

Jesus loves you . . . just because you're you!

Thank You for loving me and
wanting to be my friend.

Jesus loves me
because I'm me!

Macey Fossett, Fossett Ministries, Dalton, GA

True Wisdom Comes from God

God's wisdom is deep, and his power is great.
—JOB 9:4

Wisdom might be a hard word to understand. Wisdom is being smart, but it's a special kind of smart. Wisdom is being smart about how to live life so that God is happy and we're happy too.

When we need to make a tough decision, we may not always have the wisdom we need. Guess what? God has a lot of wisdom. He will never, ever run out of wisdom, and He will always share with us.

God will give us wisdom whenever we ask Him. He wants to help us make good choices.

Awesome God, thank You for sharing Your wisdom with me!

I can ask God to give me wisdom.

God Knows My Name

"I have called you by name, and you are mine."
—ISAIAH 43:1

Think about how much you love your favorite stuffed animal, the one that makes you smile a huge smile. You take good care of that cuddly friend, you always know where he is, and you do everything you can together.

God loves you so much more than you love your favorite stuffed animal. God loves you so much that He, the Creator of the whole universe, knows your name. And He chose you to know Him and to love Him. That's why He says you are His.

How special to be loved by God!

You know my name! God, that makes me smile! I want to be Yours forever.

God knows my name, and I am His . . . forever.

WEEK 5 • WEEKEND

Praise God, I Am One of a Kind

I praise you because you made me in an amazing and wonderful way.

—PSALM 139:14

God made you—and He only made one *you*! There is no one else anywhere who is exactly like you. He made you the perfect *you*.

God chose your hair color and your eye color, and He put your eyes, your nose, and your ears just where He wanted them to be. God made you good at certain things (maybe art or sports or music or computers). He made you like certain things (maybe reading or dancing or puppy dogs or science). God made you a beautiful person, and no one else is like you!

Dear God, I love that You made me one of a kind. I love being special to You!

I praise God I am one of a kind.

A New Baby!

Today your Savior was born in David's town. He is Christ, the Lord.

—LUKE 2:11

D o you get excited when a baby is born? You might remember the day your sister, your brother, or a cousin was born.

At Christmastime we remember when Jesus was born. Jesus was born in a stable where animals lived because there was no place else to stay. Angels sang beautiful songs to celebrate that Jesus was born. Shepherds heard about Jesus from the angels and hurried to go visit the baby.

It's always exciting when a baby is born. But Jesus being born was extra-exciting because He would save us from being punished for our sins.

Dear God, thank You for being punished for my sins. I'm glad You were born to be my Savior!

Jesus was born to be my Savior!

Deanna Hunt Carswell,
First Baptist Church Woodstock, Woodstock, GA

Sharing God's Love

God made us new people so that we would do good works.
—EPHESIANS 2:10

How do you feel when someone helps you? Maybe a teacher helps you understand math. Maybe Mom helps you learn to swim. Maybe Dad helps you with your science project.

Do you feel loved when people help you? When we help people, they feel loved. That's one reason why God wants us to help people. He calls it "doing good works." Doing nice things for people helps them feel loved. They feel your love *and* they feel God's love.

God made you to help people know that He loves them.

Dear God, thank You for choosing me to show Your love to people.

When I help others,
I show God's love.

Be Happy!

*Always be happy. Never stop praying. Give
thanks whatever happens.*
—1 Thessalonians 5:16–18

Always be happy? That's hard to do! It's hard to be happy when we have a fever or when our best friend moves away.

But we can feel happy and sad at the same time. You are sad to be sick but happy Mom takes care of you. You're sad when your friend moves, but you're happy God will take care of him.

When you feel sad, pray. Praying will remind you that God loves you. Even when we have a fever or our friend moves, we can be happy because we know that God loves us.

Dear God, help me to be happy even when my heart is sad.

I can always be happy because God loves me!

Jesus Loves Me

"For God loved the world so much that he gave his only Son."

—JOHN 3:16

D id you know that moms and dads love their babies even before the babies are born? And after babies are born, moms and dads will do anything to keep them safe.

God loves His Son, Jesus, very much too. But God let His Son go to earth in order to die. It was hard for God to let the Son He loved die on the cross.

So why did God let Jesus be born in order to die? Because God loves you, and this was the only way your sins could be forgiven.

God, thank You for loving us and sending Your only Son to die for our sins.

God gave us Jesus to show us how much He loves us!

Deanna Hunt Carswell,
First Baptist Church Woodstock, Woodstock, GA

Find Help for Decisions

The Scriptures are able to make you wise. And that wisdom leads to salvation through faith in Christ Jesus.

—2 TIMOTHY 3:15

The Bible is an amazing book that God gave us so we can know Him better.

In the Bible—also called *Scripture* and *God's Word*—God tells us how to live a life that makes Him happy and that is good for us at the same time. In other words, God gives us wisdom in the Bible so we make good decisions.

The most important decision you will make in your life will be deciding to ask Jesus to forgive you for your sins and to be your King.

That is a very wise decision!

Dear God, please help me understand the Bible so I can make good decisions.

The Bible will help me be wise!

Deanna Hunt Carswell,
First Baptist Church Woodstock, Woodstock, GA

God's Gift of Heaven

"He who believes in me will have life even if he dies."
—JOHN 11:25

Do you know for sure that you will go to heaven someday? You *can* know for sure!

The Bible tells us that God loved the world so much that he gave his only Son to die on the cross because that's the only way your sins can be forgiven. If you choose to believe that Jesus died for your sins—and that is completely true!—then you can ask Him to be your King.

Living with Jesus as King is the best way to live on earth—and it means you can be sure you'll go to heaven.

God, thank You for dying on the cross for my sins. Help me understand why that is important.

God wants me to live in heaven some day!

The Best Dad Ever!

We are God's children.
—ROMANS 8:16

Quick! Name five things that you really like. Do you know who gave you those good things—and all the other good things in your life? God did!

Like your daddy, God gives you what you need, takes care of you, watches over you, and loves you. He wants you to talk to Him (that's what praying is), and He wants you to love Him. In other words, God wants to be like a dad to you—and because He's an awesome and good and powerful God, He'll be the best Dad ever!

Dear God, I am so glad that I am Your child because You are the best Dad ever!

I am God's child!

Jesus Is Alive!

Jesus is not here. He has risen from death!
—LUKE 24:6

O ur God is amazing!

He made this beautiful world with its big oceans and tall mountains. He made trees and flowers, hippos and pandas, lizards and eagles.

He made your body to see and hear, talk and laugh, run and jump, think and learn.

The most amazing thing God did, though, happened after Jesus died on the cross. Our amazing God is completely powerful, and He did not let Jesus stay dead. Nothing is impossible for our God!

Today and every day we can be filled with joy because Jesus is alive.

Dear God, You did not let Jesus stay dead! You truly are amazing!

Jesus didn't stay dead! Jesus is alive!

Superhero Strength

The Lord's Spirit has filled me with power and strength.
—MICAH 3:8

Who is your favorite superhero? Superheroes have superpowers that make them strong in a certain way. What power does your favorite hero have?

Do you know that because you love Jesus you have a special strength too? It's from God. It won't make you able to lift an airplane, but it will give you strength to do everything you need to do. God's Spirit helps you be kind, speak the truth, obey Mom and Dad, take the spelling test, and complete your chores.

Ask God to give you the strength to do the right thing—and He will!

God, please give me strength to do the right thing even when I don't feel like it.

God shares His strength with me!

Hollie Hunt Hixson, Cross Point Church, Nashville, TN

Everywhere and Everything

He is the King of all kings and the Lord of all lords.
—1 TIMOTHY 6:15

What is the best trip you have ever taken? Where did you go? What did you like about it?

No matter where you go, even if a place is new to you, it's not new to Jesus. There is nowhere too far away for God to be. He is everywhere all the time, and that's very good news for us.

Jesus is also in charge of everything all the time. He is King of kings and Lord of lords, and that is also very good news for us. Because Jesus is in charge of everything, He will take good care of you.

Wherever you go, King Jesus is already there, and He knows just what to do.

Jesus, I am glad that You are in charge as an all-loving, all-wise, all-powerful King.

Jesus is everywhere!

God Cares

He counts the stars and names each one.
Our Lord is great and very powerful.
—Psalm 147:4–5

Read the verse for today. God knows how many stars are in the sky. Look at the sky tonight after dark. That's a lot of stars to know! And not only does God know how many stars there are, but He named them all too.

God also knows how many hairs are on your head. He knows what makes you happy. He knows your favorite book, favorite color, and favorite meal. God cares about you and every single part of your life, and because He is "great and very powerful," He does good things for you.

Thank You, great and powerful God, for caring about every detail of my life.

God cares about every part of my life!

Do the Right Thing

*Even a child is known by his behavior. His actions
show if he is innocent and good.*
—PROVERBS 20:11

Take an empty glass jar and fill it up with
something small like pebbles. Our life is like
that jar. Even though we don't fill up our lives with
pebbles, people will see what is in our lives just like
we see what is in the jar. What do you want people
to see in your life?

We fill our lives with the things we do, people we
see, and places we go. Are those things and people
and places good? Can people see God's love in
your life? We want our lives to be full of kind words
and helpful actions. Jesus will help us choose good
things.

*Jesus, please help me to fill my life with
good things, like love.*

Jesus will help me
do the right thing.

When You Are Afraid

You won't need to be afraid when you lie down.
When you lie down, your sleep will be peaceful.
—Proverbs 3:24

Most of us are afraid of something. Do spiders give you the creeps, or loud noises make your heart beat really fast? Maybe you really don't like being alone in the dark. Life is full of scary things, and all of us feel afraid at times.

But if we obey God, we do not have to fear anything—ever. God promises that He will take care of us when we meet up with a spider, wonder what the big noise was, or find ourselves alone in the dark.

God, thank You for always taking care of me so that I don't need to be afraid.

I don't need to be afraid.

44

Dr. Adam B. Dooley,
Sunnyvale First Baptist Church, Dallas, TX

Showing God You Love Him

We should worship God in a way that pleases him.
—HEBREWS 12:28

Have you ever wondered how you can show God that you love Him?

God wants us to worship Him. And *worshipping* means telling God how great He is. We do that when we pray and sing praise songs and go to church.

We also worship God when we obey what He says in the Bible, when we love others the way He does, and when we do what our parents tell us to do.

These are just a few ways you can worship God. What are other things you can do to show God you love Him?

God, I want to worship You by making You happy with everything I do.

I show God
that I love Him
by obeying.

The Best Friend You Can Have

"I became your friend because of my love and kindness."
—JEREMIAH 31:3

Have you ever met someone who was hard to be nice to? Maybe that person says mean things, refuses to share, or acts like a bully. Being friends with someone like that may seem impossible.

It takes a special person to love someone who is not very nice. Did you know God is that kind of special Person? Even though you do bad things sometimes (everyone does!), God wants to be your friend. Nothing you do will ever make God love you less. He is the best friend you can ever have!

God, thank You for being my friend even when I'm not very nice or when I make mistakes.

God loves me and wants to be my Friend.

Finding New Treasure

I am as happy over your promises as if I had
found a great treasure.

—PSALM 119:162

What treasures have you found? Maybe you've found a coin or a toy or a flower in the garden. Treasure can be so exciting!

Did you know that the Bible is full of treasure? It tells us how much God loves us and how we can make Him happy. The Bible also tells about people who loved God and obeyed Him a long, long time ago. And the Bible tells us a lot about Jesus!

The Bible has treasures like God's promises, His instructions, and stories Jesus told. That's why it's good to read the Bible every day.

God, help me love the Bible and find
treasures in it every time I read it.

Reading the Bible
helps me discover
God's treasure.

Dr. Adam B. Dooley,
Sunnyvale First Baptist Church, Dallas, TX

One Thing to Remember

God is not a human being. He does not change his mind. What he says he will do, he does. What he promises, he keeps.
—NUMBERS 23:19

H ave you ever broken a promise or told a lie? We do not always do what we say we will do, and that is breaking a promise. Unfortunately, we do not always tell the exact truth, and that is the same as telling a lie. But God does not break promises, and He always tells the truth.

Remember these truths about God: Because God is perfect, He always keeps His promises. And because God is perfect, He always tells the complete truth. So you never have to doubt what God says in His Word. Believe what He says and trust Him always.

Dear God, thank You for always keeping Your promises.

I can trust that God will keep His promises.

Dr. Adam B. Dooley,
Sunnyvale First Baptist Church, Dallas, TX

Learning to Be a Good Friend

A friend loves you all the time. A brother is
always there to help you.

—PROVERBS 17:17

What do you think makes someone a good friend?

A lot of things make someone a good friend, but maybe the most important thing is the person's willingness to love you no matter what and to encourage you when you are sad. Good friends listen when you are sad, pray when you are worried, and show up whenever you need them.

Jesus is that kind of Friend to you: He listens to you, He prays for you, and He is always with you even when you make mistakes.

Dear God, thank You for giving me friends.

Jesus is a good friend to me!

Happy Parents

*Make your father and mother happy. Give your
mother a reason to be glad.*

—Proverbs 23:25

Moms and dads love their children so much,
and children make them so happy!

You can make your mom and dad happy by
doing what they ask you to do and by trying hard
at school or with chores at home.

You make your parents happy when you obey
them. Even if you don't always do your best, your
mother and father still love you. Your parents are a
lot like God that way. God will always love you, and
you make Him happy when you
do what He says.

*Jesus, thank You for my
parents, and please help me make
them glad. Amen.*

> I will look for
> ways to make my
> parents glad.

Being Friends with Jesus

"You are my friends if you do what I command you."
—JOHN 15:14

It is so good to have friends, isn't it? Well, it is even better—it is completely amazing—that you can have Jesus as your friend!

You show Jesus that you want to be His friend when you do what He tells you to do. Jesus said, "You are my friends if you do what I command you."

The command Jesus was talking about is "Love each other as I have loved you" (v. 12). Jesus gives you that command because love is so important to Him. Jesus also helps you obey that command. And He calls you His friend!

Jesus, please help me love people as You command, and thank You for being my friend.

Both Jesus and I are happy when we spend time together.

Dr. Phil Thomas, Shiloh Baptist Church, Fort Gaines, GA

Show People You Love Jesus

You are young, but do not let anyone treat you as if you were not important. Be an example to show the believers how they should live. Show them with your words, with the way you live, with your love, with your faith, and with your pure life.

—1 TIMOTHY 4:12

D o you sometimes think people don't pay attention to you because you are young? Do they sometimes treat you like you don't know anything because you're not older? Well, God has a different idea.

God says that, no matter how old we are, we can show that we love Jesus by what we say and what we do. Being nice to a mean person and saying please and thank you are ways we can show people that Jesus is our Lord and King no matter how old or young we are.

Jesus, please help me say and do things so that others will want to know You.

I can show people
that I love Jesus.

Dr. Phil Thomas, Shiloh Baptist Church, Fort Gaines, GA

My Room in Heaven

"There are many rooms in my Father's house. I would not tell you this if it were not true. I am going there to prepare a place for you."
—JOHN 14:2

What kind of bedroom would you like if you could have any kind of bedroom?

Did you know Jesus is making a room for you in God's house in heaven? You can be sure you will like the room because God made you, so He knows what you like!

We don't know a lot of details about heaven, but we know it will be a place without sadness or tears. And we know that Jesus is making a room for you because He wants you to be there with Him!

Thank You, Jesus, for making a place in heaven just for me.

Jesus will have an amazing room for me in heaven!

My Big Family

*"My true brother and sister and mother are those
who do the things God wants."*

—MARK 3:35

How big is your family? You can count brothers and sisters. Mom or Dad can help you count aunts and uncles and cousins. Your family may be small or big. But when you get to heaven and are with other people who love Jesus, you will have a huge family!

Everyone who loves Jesus and who does what God wants them to do is in God's big family. That is lots and lots of brothers and sisters. And guess what? You all have the same loving Father!

*Jesus, thank You for letting
me be part of Your family.*

I like being in
God's family.

We Are Helpers

Then the Lord God said, "It is not good for the man to be
alone. I will make a helper who is right for him."
—GENESIS 2:18

G od the Father has never been alone. He has always had His Son, Jesus, and the Holy Spirit, and Jesus and the Holy Spirit have always had God.

When God made the very first man, God named him Adam and gave him a lot of stuff to do. God and Adam could talk, and they did. But Adam didn't have any friends who were like him, and he didn't have anyone to help him with his work, either. So God made Eve to be Adam's wife, friend, and helper.

God created us to need friends and helpers. God also wants us to be a friend and a helper to others.

Thank You, God, that I'm not alone.
Thank You for friends and helpers.

I want to be a good
friend and helper!

Dr. Phil Thomas, Shiloh Baptist Church, Fort Gaines, GA

God Takes Care of You

*My God will use his wonderful riches in Christ
Jesus to give you everything you need.*
—Philippians 4:19

Sometimes we want things we don't need. And that's okay.

Sometimes our parents or our grandparents get us the things we want but don't really need, like ice cream or an extra box of crayons. It's fun to get some of those things, isn't it? But sometimes things we want would not be good for us, and God knows that.

So God does not always let us have everything we want, but He always gives us everything we need. God loves you, and He will always take care of you by giving you all you need and some of the things you want.

Father, thank You for giving me some things I want and everything I need.

God will always
give me all I need!

Dr. Robert C. Pitman, Evangelist, Muscle Shoals, AL

Jesus and Bullies

"Treat others as you want them to treat you."
—MATTHEW 7:12 CEV

Do you know what a bully is? A bully is someone who tries to make other boys and girls do things they do not want to do. A bully is mean, a bully can be scary, and a bully can make people very, very sad.

And that makes Jesus sad. He does not want anyone to be a bully. He taught us to treat others the way we want them to treat us. That means we should be kind to others because we want people to be kind to us. When we do, we make Jesus happy.

Father, help me treat others in a way that makes You happy.

I will treat people the way I want them to treat me.

God Is My Helper

My help comes from the Lord. He made heaven and earth.
—Psalm 121:2

N o matter how old or strong or tall we become, we can't do everything all by ourselves. Sometimes we need someone to help us.

Do you know that God loves to help you? He's a good Helper to have because He can do anything! He made heaven and earth and everything else. He is big, and He is strong. He is smart and wise, so He knows the best way to help you.

If you ask God for His help, know that He will give you the best kind of help.

Dear God, every day I need Your help for many things. Thank You for helping.

My God is big enough to help me with any problem.

Getting Along with Others

Do your best to live in peace with everyone.
—ROMANS 12:18

It is good when people get along with one another, isn't it? And it is sad when people fight. God thinks so too. He does not want us to fight with one another. He wants us to do our best to live in peace.

That's why He tells us to try hard to be nice to people. Everyone is happier when no one is angry. Everyone is happier when no one is sad because of hurt feelings.

When God tells us to "live in peace," He wants us to do our best to be nice and not to fight. He will help us when we ask Him to. So let's ask Him.

Dear God, please help me be nice, and please help me not get mad. Amen.

> I want to "live in peace" with people.

Dr. Robert C. Pitman, Evangelist, Muscle Shoals, AL

Living in a Happy Land

Happy is the nation whose God is the Lord.
—PSALM 33:12

Four quick questions:
What is the name of your street? Your city? Your state? Your country?

You live on a street, in a city, in a state, in a country—and a lot of people live in this country. We don't all look alike or think alike or even speak the same language. It can be hard to get along.

The best way for all the people in one country to get along is to ask God to guide their decisions and help them make their laws. If a country lets God lead them, it will be a happy nation.

Father, thank You for the United States. Please help this country understand how important You are.

I want God to be the leader of my nation.

Dr. Robert C. Pitman, Evangelist, Muscle Shoals, AL

Making Good Choices

Patience is better than strength.
—PROVERBS 16:32

Every day you have to make choices—a lot of choices.

Sometimes making choices is easy. Most of us would choose to eat ice cream instead of spinach. That is an easy choice.

Sometimes choices are more difficult. On a sunny day, you might have to choose between pushing to the front of the line for recess or patiently waiting your turn. When you have to make a hard choice, take some time to pray and then wait for God to help you know which choice to make. He will help you.

Dear God, please help me make right choices in my life.

I want God to help me make hard choices!

My Country Is Great

Doing what is right makes a nation great.
—Proverbs 14:34

Have you ever gone with your mom or your dad to vote? If you have, you may have gotten one of those cool stickers that says, "I Voted."

Voting is important. We get to choose the people who will lead our city, our state, and our nation. It is a good idea to ask God to help us choose the right person.

The right person will help our country do what is right. When a nation does what is right, God will make that nation great.

Dear God, please help the grown-ups in my town vote for people who will help America do what is right.

I can't vote yet, but I can pray for America.

Doing What Is Right

*Happy are those people who are fair, who do
what is right at all times.*

—PSALM 106:3

Sometimes people are mean to us, and that makes us sad. Sometimes we do what we know is wrong, and then we are punished. That doesn't make us happy either.

God knows that we will only be happy when we are kind to other people and when we make the right choices.

That means being nice to your friends even when they do things that hurt your feelings. Choosing to be nice is the right choice.

When we make wise choices and do what is right, we are happy, and God is happy too.

Dear God, help me to be kind to others and to make good choices.

I am glad God
can help me do
what is right!

Ann White, In Grace Ministries, Atlanta, GA

God Listens

God has wisdom and power. He has good advice and understanding.

—JOB 12:13

God listens to you when you pray—and He loves it when you pray.

God wants to hear about everything in your life. There is nothing too big or too small for you to talk to Him about. He wants you to talk to Him about anything that makes you happy and anything that makes you sad.

You can also ask Him questions, and He will answer you. When you need help, He will help you know what to do. You can be sure that God hears your prayers and that He will answer.

God, thank You for always listening to me.

God will listen to my prayers.

Ann White, In Grace Ministries, Atlanta, GA

Choosing What Is Right

[The Lord] gives me new strength. For the good of his name, he leads me on paths that are right.

—PSALM 23:3

It's hard to follow the rules when our friends don't, isn't it?

God gave us rules to follow so we don't get hurt and so we don't hurt other people. The Bible tells us those rules and teaches what is right and what is wrong. The more we read the Bible, the more we learn about how to make God happy by how we live.

When we don't know what to do, we can ask God to help us. He will make us strong so we can choose what is right and do what is right.

God, please show me what is right and give me strength to do it.

My God helps me be strong.

Jesus Loves Me

"This is my command: Love each other as I have loved you."
—JOHN 15:12

Maybe you've heard the song that starts with "Jesus loves me! This I know, for the Bible tells me so." (Isn't that the best news ever?)

Many times in the Bible, Jesus said that He loves us. He also commanded us to love other people. It can be hard to love everybody, but Jesus helps us.

Jesus also told us to think about how much He loves us. Jesus loved us enough to die for us! We thank Him for dying on the cross by obeying Him, and we obey Him when we choose to love people.

Dear Jesus, thank You for loving me. Please help me love others.

> Jesus loves me—
> and He helps me
> love others.

Obeying God Is Right

A person who tries to live right and be loyal finds life, success and honor.

—PROVERBS 21:21

G od wants you to do what is right. That's one reason He gave us the Bible.

In the Bible, you learn how much Jesus loves you. You also learn how to be a good friend, love your family, and be kind. When you do what God tells you to do, you will have a better life. That's why God gave us the rules!

Sometimes obeying God will not be easy, but it is always the best thing to do. Pray and ask God to help you.

Obeying God is always right!

Dear God, please help me obey Your commands and show You that I love You.

I want to obey God!

Ann White, In Grace Ministries, Atlanta, GA

Giving the Gift of Love

*We all have different gifts. Each gift came
because of the grace that God gave us.*
—ROMANS 12:6

You probably like to get gifts. That can be very fun. But giving gifts is exciting too. Something special and wonderful happens in our hearts when we give.

The best gifts to give, though, are not toys. God gives us amazing gifts like being able to teach, lead, encourage, and serve. God also gives the gift of love, and giving love is better than giving toys. God is pleased when we give a hug, a kind word, or a helping hand.

Who will you give some of God's love to today?

*God, thank You for giving me Your love.
Help me give Your love to others.*

The best gift I
can give anyone
is love!

Pastor Jeff Crook,
Blackshear Place Baptist Church, Flowery Branch, GA

Share the Good News!

How beautiful on the mountains are the feet of those who bring good news.

—ISAIAH 52:7 NIV

Sometimes we run to share good news, like "It's snowing!"

You have good news about Jesus to share too! (The fancy name for that news is "the gospel.") The good news is that God loves us so much that He sent His Son, Jesus, to take the punishment for our sins. Jesus did that by dying on the cross. Jesus did not stay dead. He rose from the dead, He forgives our sins, and we will live with Him in heaven one day.

Wherever your feet take you, you can tell others this good news that Jesus loves them.

God, please help me share the good news that Jesus loves me and died for my sins.

I can share the good news every day!

It's Good to Have a Friend!

Two people are better than one. They get more done by working together.

—ECCLESIASTES 4:9

Some people have a best friend. Some people have a lot of friends. Some of us know Jesus, and He is our friend too.

The Bible tells us that friends are good to have because they can help us.

When you are sad, a friend will cheer you up. When you are lonely, you can call a friend. If you have to do something hard, a friend can help you. Friends can also pray for each other.

It is good to thank God for giving you friends—and it is very good to pray for them.

God, thank You for my friends. Please bless them—and help me be a good friend.

I am glad that God gives me friends.

Patience and Love

Try to understand each other. Love each other as brothers.
—1 PETER 3:8

It happens to all of us. We get upset with friends. We get angry with our family.

The next time that happens to you, do what God says. He tells us in the Bible to be patient with others and to keep loving people even when they make us mad.

All of us are sinners. That means all of us need people to be patient and loving with us. So instead of saying mean things when you are upset, you can choose to be patient and loving just like God is patient and loving to you.

*Lord, thank You for Your patience and love.
Please help me be patient and love others.*

> I want to be
> patient and loving.

Just Ask!

If any of you needs wisdom, you should ask God for it.
—JAMES 1:5

D id you know you can ask God anything? Maybe you need to make a choice, but you don't know what to do. You can ask God!

God is wise. That means He always knows the best thing for you to do—and He wants you to know what that best thing is! But He wants you to ask.

God gives us wisdom when we ask Him for wisdom. Wisdom helps us know what to do about a problem or a decision. When you ask, God will give you the wisdom you need.

Just ask.

God, thank You for always giving me wisdom when I ask You for it.

When I need help with a problem, I will ask God.

Pastor Jeff Crook,
Blackshear Place Baptist Church, Flowery Branch, GA

Do You Need Any Help?

When we have the opportunity to help anyone, we should do it.
—GALATIANS 6:10

One day a lot of people were listening to Jesus teach, and Jesus knew they were hungry. What could they eat?

One of Jesus' friends found a boy who had five loaves and two fish. But how could one boy's lunch feed this huge crowd? Nothing is impossible for Jesus: He made a lot of food from that small lunch. Everyone ate—and there were leftovers!

God can do big things even when we help in small ways. So who will you help? Ask your parents to help you find people who need help.

Dear God, please show me who to help today.

I want to help
one person
every day.

Created to Work

The Lord God put the man in the garden of Eden to care for it and work it.

—GENESIS 2:15

Do you have chores to do around the house? In the Bible, Adam had chores to do too. Adam was the first man God created. Adam's big job was to care for the Garden of Eden, and that meant lots of little chores like weeding, picking fruit from the trees, and making sure the animals that lived there were healthy.

God gave us brains and muscles so we could work, and it is good for us to work. When we work, we can help others. When we do a good job, we please God.

Dear God, help me be a good worker so that I will please You.

I want to work with a happy heart!

Shhh! It's a Secret!

"When you give to the poor, give very secretly....
Your giving should be done in secret."
—MATTHEW 6:3-4

Jesus is happy when His followers share what they have with people who are poor. He is even happier when we give those gifts in secret.

Jesus is sad when people give gifts just so others will see them. Jesus wants us to give because it is a way to share His love. He also knows that giving to people makes us happy—and that giving to people in secret makes us even happier.

Maybe your family can give something to people who have less than you do this week. Shhh! Keep it a secret!

Dear God, I don't want to brag when I give. I know that You will see my gift. You will bless me when I give.

I want to give
without bragging.

Love God!

Love the Lord your God with all your heart, soul and strength.

—DEUTERONOMY 6:5

God created a beautiful world for us, and He knew that we would have a lot in this world to love. We love flowers and puppies and horses. We love the mountains and the beach. We love the twinkling stars and the warm sun. We love movies and books and baseball and soccer. We love our family and our friends.

Yes, we have a lot to love, but God told us what to love most: "Love the Lord your God with all your heart, soul and strength." We need to love God most of all.

Dear God, help me to always love You with all I have.

I want to always love God most of all!

Dan and Debbie Kubish, NewSpring Church, Wichita, KS

Happy Helpers

Whoever helps others will himself be helped.
—PROVERBS 11:25

Toby and his family had just finished dinner. Mom began to clear the table, and Toby decided to help her. He carried a dish to the sink. Then he got another dish and a glass. Toby's mom smiled and thanked Toby for helping. Then Toby smiled. It made Toby happy to help his mom.

Helping someone makes that person feel good. Helping someone makes you feel good too. And God is happy when you help others.

It is nice to know how to make God happy! Who will you help today?

Dear God, help me be a happy helper who makes You happy.

I want to be a happy helper!

What Time Is It?

There is a right time for everything. Everything on earth has its special season. —Ecclesiastes 3:1

What is your favorite time of year? What do you like about that time?

Summer is a good time for vacation. Autumn is a good time for learning. During the winter, we celebrate Jesus' birth at Christmas, and in some places it snows. In the spring, new flowers grow, and we celebrate Easter when Jesus died on the cross and then rose from the dead!

God made all four seasons—summer, autumn, winter, and spring. God also made day and night. He made play time and rest time.

God made a right time for everything to happen.

Dear God, thank You for making things happen at just the right time!

I know that God's timing is perfect.

Always!

"You can be sure that I will be with you always. I will continue with you until the end of the world."
—MATTHEW 28:20

When Josie's parents went on a trip, Josie got to stay with her grandparents. Every night Josie and her parents talked to each other on the phone. Mom and Dad asked Josie about her day. They told her how much they loved her. They reminded her that they would be home soon.

When Jesus went back home to heaven, His friends talked to Him by praying. Jesus told His friends that He would always love them, guide them, teach them, and protect them. Jesus is with us too. We can talk to Him in prayer.

God, I'm glad You will always guide me, teach me, protect me, and love me. Always!

Jesus will always be with me.

Dan and Debbie Kubish, NewSpring Church, Wichita, KS

God's Grace!

People are made right with God by his grace,
which is a free gift.

—ROMANS 3:24

God loves us! And God wants us to love Him and to love people. But we don't always do a good job, and that's called *sin*.

But Jesus loves perfectly, and He never sinned. So He took the punishment for our sins by dying on the cross. But He didn't stay dead. He rose, and now our sins are forgiven when we trust Him, even though we deserved to be punished. That is called *grace*.

Now we can be in God's family and even call Him "Father"—and this is wonderful news.

Dear God, thank You for giving us grace so we can know and love You.

Jesus gave me an incredible gift.

Dr. James Merritt, Cross Pointe Church, Duluth, GA

Knowing and Loving

"God even knows how many hairs are on your head."
—MATTHEW 10:30

Can you imagine counting every single hair on your head? That would be a very hard job, but it's not too hard for God.

Think about people you know. Some people have a lot of hair, and some don't! But God knows the number of hairs on every person's head, whether they have a lot or a little.

God also knows your name, what you like to do and eat and read, what you are afraid of, and what you want to be when you grow up. God knows everything about you because He made you. And, yes, He loves you!

Thank You, God, for knowing every single thing about me— and loving me anyway!

God loves me and knows everything about me!

Unending Love

The Lord's love never ends. His mercies never stop. They are new every morning.
—LAMENTATIONS 3:22–23

Most good things end, don't they? Birthday parties, roller coaster rides, and vacations all end. But God's love will never end! His love goes on and on, forever and ever. God will never stop loving you!

God loves you on your best days, and God loves you on your worst days. He loves you when you are happy, and He loves you when you are sad. He even loves you when you feel unlovable or you've made bad choices. God loves you every single minute of every single day—and He'll never stop!

Dear God, thank You for never stopping loving me.

God will never stop loving me!

God Gave His Son

God let even his own Son suffer for us. God gave his Son for us all. So with Jesus, God will surely give us all things.
—ROMANS 8:32

What is the best gift you think you have ever received? The greatest gift God has given us is Jesus!

God let Jesus come to earth to be punished for our sins. That must have been the hardest gift anyone ever gave away. But God gave the gift of Jesus because He loves you and me so much. He knew that we couldn't be in His family if He didn't let Jesus die and then rise from the dead.

No gift is as amazing as God's gift of His Son. Since God gave that gift, He will surely give us anything else we need.

Dear God, thank You for giving us Your Son and for all Your blessings.

God will be sure I have what I need every day!

Dr. James Merritt, Cross Pointe Church, Duluth, GA

God's Great Goodness

You are wonderful, and while everyone watches, you store up blessings for all who honor and trust you.
—PSALM 31:19 CEV

We can measure how tall you are, how much the dog weighs, and how much flour we need to bake a cake. But we can't measure God's love or His wisdom or His goodness.

God is very good—and He doesn't keep that goodness all to Himself. God shares His goodness with you and me and everyone on earth. God has goodness for all people—goodness like strawberries, sunshine, and friends. But God has special goodness for people who love Jesus: God forgives our sins and makes a place for us in heaven.

God is so good!

Thank You, God, for being good to everyone and especially good to us who love You.

I'm glad God shares His goodness with me!

Dr. James Merritt, Cross Pointe Church, Duluth, GA

Pray More, Worry Less

"Don't worry about tomorrow."
—MATTHEW 6:34

Jesus tells us not to worry. But what is worry? We are worrying when we think and think and think about our problems instead of praying to God and asking Him to help us.

All of us have worried before, but Jesus told us not to worry about anything. Jesus told us that, instead of worrying, we can pray and tell God all that we are thinking and feeling.

God has always met every single need you and I have had, and He will keep meeting every need. You don't have to worry!

Jesus, thank You for being in control of everything, and I don't need to worry.

God takes care of me!

What Is Faith?

*Faith means being sure of the things we hope for.
And faith means knowing that something is real
even if we do not see it.*

—HEBREWS 11:1

We can't see the air we breathe, but we know it's real and that it keeps us alive.

We can't see Jesus, but we know that His love is real and that He keeps us safe.

The Bible also says that God will love you no matter what—even when you disobey or mess up—and that He has good plans for your life. We can't see those things, but we know the Bible is true, and God always does what He says He will do.

Faith is believing God.

Jesus, help me to have faith that You love me and will always love me.

God always does what He says He will do.

Depend on God

Depend on the Lord. Trust him, and he will take care of you. Then your goodness will shine like the sun.
— Psalm 37:5–6

God loves us so much, and we show Him that we love Him when we trust Him with our whole heart. If we depend on Him, He will help us do what is right. And what He wants us to do is always right.

When we do what is right, when we obey God, and when we depend on Him instead of being worried or afraid, other people will notice. If they ask us why we're doing what we're doing or why we aren't worrying, we can tell them about God and how much He loves them too.

Dear God, thank You for being a God I can depend on.

I want to talk to people about Jesus.

Our Big God

*God, your thoughts are precious to me. They are
so many! If I could count them, they would be
more than all the grains of sand.*

—Psalm 139:17–18

Are you like me? I'm amazed by how much
doctors know about eyes, ears, tummies, and
bones. I'm also amazed by how much mechanics
know about trucks and cars and motorcycles.

Even though those people know a lot about their
jobs, our God knows a lot more about life—a lot
more about everything!—than we do. God knows
everything about everything. Even the smartest
human being can't understand God's thoughts and
ideas or even be able to count them all.

I like having a very big, very smart God!

*Lord, You are big and powerful
and smart—and I love You!*

God knows
everything
about my life!

Dr. Grant Ethridge, Liberty Baptist Church, Hampton, VA

God's Great Care

"When birds are sold, two small birds cost only a penny.... You are worth much more than many birds."
—MATTHEW 10:29, 31

Sparrows, crows, parrots, blue jays, robins, peacocks, ostriches—think about how many birds live in this world. We could never count them all! And you know what? The Bible says that God cares so much about the birds that nothing bad happens to one of them without Him knowing. Not a single one!

God cares about the birds, but He cares a lot more about you. God cares about every part of your life, and He knows everything about you. No one loves you more than God does, not even your mom or grandma!

Jesus, thank You for caring so much about me!

Jesus loves me more than I can understand.

God Sees You

God watches where people go. He sees every step they take.
—JOB 34:21

Do you want to know what a hard job would be? Counting all the people who live in your city! An even harder job would be counting all the people living in America!

Those would be tough jobs for us, but they're not hard for God. That's because God is a big God, and He knows everyone, not just in America, but in the whole world!

Even though God knows so many people, He also knows you. There may be a lot of people in the world, but *you* are special to God! God sees you.

God, there are a lot of people in the world! Thank You that You see me!

I am special to God.

God's Great Love

I am sure that nothing can separate us from the love God has for us.

—ROMANS 8:38

Sometimes we aren't able to be with people who love us. (That's what *separated* means: being away from someone or something.) It can be sad to be separated from someone you care about.

But did you know that nothing—*nothing!*—can separate you from God's love? There is no place you can go where He can't love you. There is nothing you can do that would make God stop loving you. God's love can never be taken away from you. And God will never run out of love for you either! That's great news, isn't it?

Father, thank You for Your great love that is with me always.

Nothing can separate me from God's love.

Dr. Grant Ethridge, Liberty Baptist Church, Hampton, VA

I Am God's Lamb

The Lord takes care of his people like a shepherd. He gathers the people like lambs in his arms. He carries them close to him.
—Isaiah 40:11

Have you ever seen sheep calmly eating grass? They are calm because they know someone is watching out for them. The person who watches over them and takes care of them is called a shepherd.

In the Bible, Jesus calls us sheep, and He calls Himself our Shepherd. That means Jesus watches over you and takes care of you.

Now think about someone you love picking you up and hugging you. It makes you feel happy and safe and warm, doesn't it? God wants His love for you to feel that way too.

Thank You, Jesus, for loving me and making me feel happy, safe, and warm.

God is my Shepherd and watches over me.

Pam Mercer, CrossLife Church, Oviedo, FL

Thank You, God!

Pray and ask God for everything you need. And when you pray, always give thanks.
—PHILIPPIANS 4:6

Praying is talking to God. And you can tell Him anything you want to tell Him. You can also ask Him to give you things you need. And it's good to give thanks—to thank God for hearing your prayers and for loving you—when you ask God for something.

God is like a very good father. He will take care of you. He will be sure you have food to eat and clothes to wear.

When God gives you something you asked Him for, it is important to thank Him for giving you what you need.

Thank You, God, for hearing my prayers and giving me everything I need.

I want to remember to always say, "Thank You, God!"

You're Not Too Little

The Lord will bless those who respect him, from the smallest to the greatest.

—Psalm 115:13 NCV

Did you know that you can do very big things for God? You can pray. You can show people God's love by helping them. You can tell people about Jesus. You can tell God how much you love Him (that's called worship). You can share your money to help people who need food. You can respect God—and that means making Him the most important part of your life!

God will bless everyone "from the smallest to the greatest" who respects Him—and that includes you. You're not too little to do big things for God!

Thank You, God, for helping me do big things for You.

I'm not big, but God can help me do big things!

What Do You Think?

The Lord knows what is in every person's mind.
He understands everything you think.
—1 CHRONICLES 28:9

Did you know that God knows everything? God knows how airplanes stay in the air and how your eyes can see. God knows what is on top of the tallest mountain and what is in the deepest part of the ocean. God knows why seeds grow and why bears sleep all winter. He even knows what you think before you say it!

God knows when you think about things that make you sad. He knows when you are thinking happy thoughts. You can turn sad thoughts into happier thoughts when you think about God and how much He loves you.

Thank You, God, for creating my brain.
Help me to think about You a lot.

The best thing I can think about is God!

Pam Mercer, CrossLife Church, Oviedo, FL

Love Is the Greatest

Three things continue forever: faith, hope and love. And the greatest of these is love.
—1 CORINTHIANS 13:13

Flowers don't last long. Puppies don't stay puppies for very long. Vacations don't last long enough. But there are three things that will last forever: faith, hope, and love.

Faith is believing that God made you, that God loves you, and that Jesus died on the cross as punishment for your sins. Hope is knowing God will keep the promises He made when the time is right. And love is caring so much about people that you will do anything for them.

God loves you, and His love for you will "continue forever."

God, thank You for the gifts of faith and hope and—greatest of all—love.

> Loving God is the most important thing I can do!

Pam Mercer, CrossLife Church, Oviedo, FL

Enjoying What I Have

*I have learned to be satisfied with the things I
have and with everything that happens.*
—PHILIPPIANS 4:11

When you enjoy what you have—when you enjoy whatever God has given you—you will have a peaceful, warm feeling inside. That is being satisfied or being content.

Sometimes knowing what your friends have makes it hard to be satisfied with what you have. When that happens, tell God you are sorry you aren't happy with what He has given you. Ask Him to teach you to be satisfied with what He has given. Ask Him to make your heart thankful.

✨ *Thank You, God, for what You give
me. Help me learn to be satisfied.* ✨

I want to learn to
enjoy what God
has given me.

No Hide and Seek

I love those who love me. Those who want me find me.
—Proverbs 8:17

Sometimes in stories, trains talk and animals talk. In today's key verse, the writer is pretending that wisdom can talk.

We learn here that if we want wisdom—if we want to be wise—God will help us be wise. Wisdom will not play hide-and-seek. Getting wisdom is simpler than playing hide-and-seek. The Bible says, "If any of you needs wisdom, you should ask God for it. . . . God will give you wisdom" (James 1:5).

All of us need wisdom, and we can ask God for it.

Thank You, God, that You will give me wisdom when I ask You for it.

I am glad that God can help me be wise!

Playing Together in Peace

It is good and pleasant when God's people live together in peace!

—PSALM 133:1

Playing with friends, playing with Dad and Mom, playing with brothers and sisters—those times can be lots of fun. But the fun will end if we start to argue or fight with one another. God doesn't want us to argue or fight!

God wants us to get along with one another. So if we are going to make God happy, we need to do whatever we can to "live together [and play together] in peace." Sharing, taking turns, and saying "I'm sorry" will help us play together in peace, and that peace will please God.

Lord, help me share, take turns, and live together with my friends and my family in peace.

I want God to be happy with the way I play!

Miss Anne Chenault, First Baptist Church, Chipley, FL 99

Help Me Understand

Help me understand, so I can obey your
teachings. I will obey them with all my heart.
—PSALM 119:34

I f you are going to obey God, you need to know what He wants you to do. You don't have to guess. The Bible tells you.

We understand the commands "Love God" and "Love your neighbor." But sometimes the Bible is hard to understand. That's when you can pray and ask God to help you understand. You can go to church and learn more about God and what He wants you to do. You can talk to your Sunday school teacher, your pastor, or your parents. God wants you to understand, and He will help you.

God, help me understand what You want
me to do so I can obey You.

God can help
me when I don't
understand.

Miss Anne Chenault, First Baptist Church, Chipley, FL

Choose Happiness

Help me obey your commands because that makes me happy.
—PSALM 119:35

What are some things that make you happy? Chocolate chip pancakes? A good book? Having a sleepover at your friend's house?

The Bible says that obeying God's commands will make you happy.

Too many people think that they will only be happy if they can do anything they want to. The Bible tells us that they are not right.

God created us, so He knows the commands we need. That's why following God's commands will make us happy: those commands are good for us.

So choose to be happy by choosing to obey God.

God, help me obey Your commands because I know they are good for me.

I am going to obey God!

Getting the Prize

You know that in a race all the runners run. But only one gets the prize. So run like that. Run to win!
—1 Corinthians 9:24

When you run in a race, do you like to win? Only one person can win—and to win you have to run and run fast.

The Bible tells us to run to win! But God is not just talking about winning a race. He is telling you and me to do our very best all the time. In anything and everything we do, we are to do our very best.

When you try your hardest, you will please God. And knowing that you pleased God is a wonderful prize!

God, please help me always do my very best in everything I do.

When I do my best, I make God happy!

Kindness for Free

Do not use your freedom as an excuse to do evil.
Live as servants of God.

—1 PETER 2:16

A dog without a leash can run where he knows he shouldn't go, or he can do what will please his master.

We have the same choice. God has forgiven our sins; we are free from punishment. Will we run where we know we shouldn't go by doing what we know we shouldn't do, or will we choose to please our Lord?

God's Word tells us we are free *not* to do bad things but to live as His servants. We serve God when we are kind or helpful or patient, when we pray for people, and when we tell people about Jesus.

God, help me choose to use my freedom to serve people and please You.

> I can serve God by
> serving others.

Miss Anne Chenault, First Baptist Church, Chipley, FL

Do You Say "Yes Sir" and "No Sir"?

Show respect for all people. Love the brothers and sisters of God's family.

—1 PETER 2:17

R espect means treating people well because we know God loves them. Every person we meet is important and valuable because all people are made by God.

There are a lot of simple ways to show respect. Saying please and thank you are ways we show people respect. If Mom or Dad asks us to do something, we do it. That is showing respect. Treating people well and speaking to them in a nice voice is also showing respect. When we treat others the way we want to be treated, we are showing them respect—and pleasing God.

Dear God, please help me show respect for others, especially for my family.

I will respect all people.

Dennis Nunn,
Every Believer a Witness Ministries, Dallas, GA

Do You Like to Sing?

Sing and make music in your hearts to the Lord.
—Ephesians 5:19

Cole didn't think he had a good singing voice. Sometimes it was a little squeaky—and his brother had once called him "Froggy." So he didn't sing much.

But God tells us to sing. It is one of His commands in the Bible.

One day Cole sang a song to God, and he could feel in his heart that God liked it! God likes hearing you sing too. He doesn't care how good—or bad—your voice is. He only cares about whether you mean the words you sing to Him.

God loves you. He wants you to sing to Him.

Dear God, thank You for loving me and wanting me to sing to You.

The best songs are the ones I sing to God.

How Powerful Is God?

Praise the Lord's glory and power.
—Psalm 29:1

There are a lot of reasons we can praise God! King David wrote that we should praise God for His glory and power—and our God is very, very powerful. God is more powerful than the oceans. He is more powerful than lightning and thunder. He is more powerful than winds on the desert.

How do we know that God is more powerful than all these things? Because He made them all! God made everything.

We can praise God because He is the Creator, because He is a great God, and because He is so powerful!

Dear God, thank You for being my powerful God!

I will praise my powerful and good God!

How Strong Are You?

I can do all things through Christ because he gives me strength.

—PHILIPPIANS 4:13

W ouldn't it be great to be able to pick up huge rocks like your favorite superhero can? But our bodies are all shapes and sizes, and not everyone has big muscles.

God cares more about how strong we are on the inside than how strong our arm muscles are. Being strong inside means being able to say no when someone wants us to do something that is wrong. Being strong inside means being able to say yes when God wants us to do something hard.

And when we need help being strong inside, God will give us His strength.

Dear God, thank You for giving me the strength I need to be strong inside.

I want to be
strong inside.

Dennis Nunn,
Every Believer a Witness Ministries, Dallas, GA

Do You Obey Your Parents?

"Honor your father and mother."
—MATTHEW 19:19

You probably have already learned that God wants you to obey your parents. When they tell you to do something, you should do it. That's pretty easy to understand.

But God wants children to do something else as they obey their parents. God wants children to obey without arguing or complaining. Children honor their parents when they don't talk back or argue with them. Even when your parents tell you to do something that you don't want to do, you make God happy—and you make your parents happy—when you obey without fussing.

Dear God, please help me honor my parents by doing what they tell me to do without fussing.

God wants me to please my parents!

Dennis Nunn,
Every Believer a Witness Ministries, Dallas, GA

Are You Selfish?

Do everything for the glory of God.
—1 CORINTHIANS 10:31

T he apostle Paul wrote today's verse to people who were very selfish. They did whatever they wanted to do, even at church. They only cared about themselves.

But God wants us to be different. He wants us to always behave in a way that will cause people to know God is good. That is what "Do everything for the glory of God" means. When we are kind, people can know God is kind. When we are patient or giving or unselfish, people will see that God is patient, generous, and unselfish. And God gets glory.

Dear God, help me do things that will make people know You are great.

I want God to get all the glory.

Helpers

You have been my help from the day I was born. I will always praise you.

—PSALM 71:6

Moms and dads are the best! They always help us when we cannot do things by ourselves. When we are babies, they feed us and change our clothes. They teach us to walk and talk and brush our teeth. Later they help us with our reading and math and riding a bike. When we have a problem, we should ask Mom or Dad for help.

The Bible tells us that God has always been around to help you when you need Him—and He always will be around to help. He loves to help you because He loves you!

God, thank You that You help me whenever I need help! I love You!

I am glad God is my Helper.

Just Do It!

Let us think about each other and help each other
to show love and do good deeds.
—HEBREWS 10:24

D id someone do something nice for you today? Did someone fix you dinner? Help you with your schoolwork? Say something loving to you? Be thankful.

Not everyone is nice! That's why God has to tell us to be thoughtful, to help each other, and to think about other people and not just ourselves.

Maybe you know a person who needs someone to be nice, or who needs to have a friend. What can you do to be kind? Do something special for that person. You'll be showing God's love.

God, You are so good to me. Help me be good to someone every day.

> I want to think
> about others
> instead of myself!

Dr. Mike Whitson,
First Baptist Church Indian Trail, Indian Trail, NC

Life-Giving Water

"I will give free water from the spring of the water of life to anyone who is thirsty."

—REVELATION 21:6

Humans can't live very long if they don't drink enough water. Those hot days—when we get sweaty and tired and thirsty, and when our mouths are so dry we can hardly swallow, remind us that we need water. Have you ever drank a glass of ice-cold water that tasted really, really good? Maybe you said, "Aaahhhh!" Then, after you drank the water, you were ready to go back out and play some more, weren't you?

Just like water can give us new energy for our body, God can give us new energy for loving Him because He offers life-giving water.

Thank You, Jesus, for energy to love You and for giving me the water of life.

Jesus gives me life-giving water for my heart.

Dr. Mike Whitson,
First Baptist Church Indian Trail, Indian Trail, NC

God Sees Us

"Whoever helps one of these little ones because they are my followers will truly get his reward."
—MATTHEW 10:42

God is happy when we do good things. And actions don't have to be big to be good!

God always sees when we do little things that are good, and He smiles. When we share with someone who does not have much, He is happy. When we say kind things to others, He is glad. When we help our neighbor by getting her mail, God is glad we are sharing His love.

What little things can you do to make God smile? He will see whatever you do—and He will be proud of you.

Father, every day please help me do something nice for someone.

God is happy when I help others.

What We Say Matters!

Like a fountain of water, the words of a good person give life.
—Proverbs 10:11

Have you heard someone say, "Sticks and stones may break my bones, but words will never hurt me"? The first part is true: sticks and stones can break bones. The second part is not true: words can hurt people!

You can probably think of a time when words made you sad. Maybe a classmate was rude, your sister was mean, or a friend was impatient.

Words can hurt people, so we need to be careful. Words are powerful. They can make people happy or sad. We want our words to make people happy. That's why God can help us!

God, please help me choose words that make people happy and always please You.

I need to be careful with my words.

What Is God Like?

"I am the Lord. The Lord is a God who shows mercy and is kind. The Lord doesn't become angry quickly. The Lord has great love and faithfulness."

—Exodus 34:6

God wants you to love Him. (Isn't that cool?) But it's hard to love someone you don't know very well, isn't it? God wants you to know Him. That's why He tells us in the Bible what He is like.

Today's verse tells us that God is kind, slow to get angry, and full of love. God sounds pretty easy to love, doesn't He?

When we are cranky or mean or disobedient, we aren't easy to love, but God keeps loving us.

Learn more about God's love for you by reading the Bible.

God, I praise You for being kind, gracious, and full of love. I love You!

I am so glad God loves me—and I love Him.

Dr. Mike Whitson,
First Baptist Church Indian Trail, Indian Trail, NC

God Leads Me

Guide me in your truth. Teach me, my God, my Savior. I trust you all day long.

—PSALM 25:5

Have you ever been in a big crowd of people who were taller than you? When you are small, it is good to have Mom or Dad hold your hand. And it is very good that they are tall. They can see what you cannot, and they can help you get where you need to go. God is like that!

God sees things you can't see, He knows everything that will happen in your life, and He can help you get where you need to go. He will guide you; He asks you to trust and follow Him.

Dear God, thank You that You will show me the way I should go.

I want God to guide me, and I will follow.

Norma Bowers, Flint-Groves Baptist Church, Gastonia, NC

The Right Way to Live

Tell them the right way to live and what they should do.
—EXODUS 18:20

Think about a time when you got a new game. Someone had to teach you how to play the game. They had to teach you the rules you needed to follow. When you learned the rules, then you knew the right way to play.

Just like there is a right way to play a game, there is a right way to live. And, like the page of rules that come with a new game, the Bible tells us "the right way to live and what [we] should do." It's good to know where to find the rules for life!

God, help me know the Bible so I know the right way to live.

> I want to learn God's rules for my life.

God's Family

*All of you together are the body of Christ. Each
one of you is a part of that body.*
—1 CORINTHIANS 12:27

The T-ball season was over. Gracie, the right fielder, was sad. She didn't think she had helped the team as much as the pitcher or first baseman had. But then Coach handed her a trophy and said, "I'm so glad you're part of this team, Gracie! You helped us win the championship!"

God's family is like a team: we all play different positions, and they're all important. God's family is also like a body: arms, legs, eyes, and noses are different from each other, but we need them all.

*Jesus, thank You for making
me part of Your family and giving
me a special job to do.*

I love being on
God's team!

When I Am Scared

*Even if I walk through a very dark valley, I will
not be afraid because you are with me.*
—PSALM 23:4

A lex cried, "Mommy, I don't like this! It is too dark!"

Alex was afraid of the dark, so he had trouble falling asleep. His mom had an idea.

"Alex, I am going to put a nightlight outside my door. Its light will come into your room, and you will know that I am right there. You don't have to be afraid."

Alex's mom was near Alex when he was afraid. And guess what? Jesus is always near, even when you feel afraid. He is always with you because He loves you.

*Jesus, thank You for being with me
whenever I feel nervous or afraid.*

I am so glad
that Jesus is
always with me!

Norma Bowers, Flint-Groves Baptist Church, Gastonia, NC   119

God Is Your Friend

The Lord is good. He gives protection in times of
trouble. He knows who trusts in him.

—NAHUM 1:7

Have you ever had a really bad day? Maybe someone said something mean or you were late to school. Maybe you got sick and had to miss a birthday party or you forgot to take your homework to school.

Whenever we have a bad day—for whatever reasons—we need a friend. A really good friend to have on a bad day is God. He knows what is going on, and He knows that you need Him. Even on your really bad days, you can know that God is good, and He will take care of you.

Lord, thank You for being my friend
on bad days and good days!

God is good, and
I can trust Him!

Norma Bowers, Flint-Groves Baptist Church, Gastonia, NC

God's Plans for You

"I have good plans for you. . . . I plan to give you hope and a good future."

—JEREMIAH 29:11

Before a new baby is born, a mom and dad have a lot of things to get ready for that tiny person. They already love that little baby, and they want to have everything the baby needs.

God loves you just like that mom and dad love their baby. God knows what you need today and what you will need as you get older. And He has good things ready for your life. That's His promise!

God loves you, and He will give you everything you need.

Thank You, Lord, for loving me and having good things ready for my life.

God has good things planned for my life.

Love Everyone!

Keep on loving each other as brothers in Christ.
Remember to welcome strangers into your homes.
—Hebrews 13:1–2

Have your parents ever invited someone over to the house whom you didn't know? Maybe that was a little scary, but your mom and dad were obeying God. He wants us to love people who love Him even if we don't know them very well.

God tells us that we need to love people who love Him as much as we love our own brothers and sisters. We love people with our actions—even if we don't know them very well—when we treat them nicely and we are kind to them. That makes God happy.

Dear God, thank You for loving me and for helping me love others.

God will help me love everyone!

Listen to the Lord

Wisdom begins with respect for the Lord. Those who obey his orders have good understanding.
—Psalm 111:10

Have you ever met a soldier who was in the military? Soldiers are trained to be strong and brave, but all soldiers have a person who is in charge of them. That person tells them exactly what they need to do, and the soldiers do it. They don't argue. They obey immediately. It is important for their safety that they obey.

The Bible tells us that we need to listen to God and do what He tells us to do. God is in charge of us, and He watches out for our safety. Like soldiers, we are not to argue, and we are to obey immediately. We show God respect when we obey Him.

God, please teach me to hear Your instructions and do what You tell me to do.

I will listen and obey God!

Christian Lloyd, First Baptist Church Lawton, Lawton, OK

Make Friends!

Live together in peace with each other. Do not be proud,
but make friends with those who seem unimportant.
—ROMANS 12:16

When Jake was a kid, he had some good friends at school, and they were together all the time. They did everything together. Then a new kid moved to their city and started coming to their school. Jake's friends and he met the new kid. He became part of their group, and he became Jake's best friend!

God tells us that we need to make friends with people who may not have a lot of friends. Ask God to help you notice who really needs a friend—and then make a new friend.

Dear God, help me make friends with someone who really needs a friend.

I will be friendly to everyone.

Christian Lloyd, First Baptist Church Lawton, Lawton, OK

Take Care!

A good man takes care of his animals.
—PROVERBS 12:10

Chris has a big, furry dog named Samson. Ally has a hamster who loves cucumbers. And Taylor's cat, Tinker Bell, likes belly rubs.

God created you. God also created dogs, hamsters, and cats. God wants us to take care of everything that He has made, and *everything* includes animals! Do you have an animal at home? What do you do to take care of it?

When we take care of animals, we show God that we are thankful for all that He has made.

Dear Lord, help me take good care of Your creation, especially the animals at my house.

I will take care of everything that God has made!

You Have a Friend in Me

A real friend will be more loyal than a brother.
—PROVERBS 18:24

Do you have a best friend, someone you do everything with, someone who is always by your side?

God tells us that He is an even closer friend than your best friend. And God says He will be a better friend than even a brother can be.

Also no matter what is going on and no matter what time of day or night it is, you can talk to God. That's really cool, isn't it? You usually can't do that with brothers and other friends.

Take some time today to talk to God, your friend.

God, I'm glad I can talk to You about everything and go to You for help.

I can talk to God like He's my best friend!

Be Kind to Everyone

Try to live in peace with all people.
—HEBREWS 12:14

D o you like it when someone is angry or unhappy with you? That does not feel good—and that is why God tells us to "try to live in peace with all people."

When we are nice to everyone we meet, we help people live in peace. Even if someone is not very nice to us, God wants us to be kind anyway. God can help you learn to be kind to people even when it is not easy.

God loves everyone in the entire world, and everyone we meet is special to God. So let's try our best to be kind!

Dear God, please help me to be nice to everyone around me, not just to my friends.

I will try to be nice to everyone.

Do Your Best

She does her work with energy. . . . She makes sure
that what she makes is good.
—Proverbs 31:17–18

Have you ever been told to do something that you don't especially want to do? That happens to all of us—even Mom and Dad. Maybe you don't want to clean your room or do your homework, and Mom and Dad don't want to clean out the garage or wash the car.

Did you know that God wants us to do our very best no matter what we are doing, and even if we don't especially want to do that thing? We make God happy when we do our best.

Dear God, help me always do my
best at everything I do.

I will always try
to do a good job.

Dr. Patrick Latham, First Baptist Church Lawton, Lawton, OK

Stop and Listen!

Remember what you are taught. And listen carefully to words of knowledge.

—PROVERBS 23:12

Think about being in the kitchen with your mom. She tells you, "Make sure not to touch this pan. It is still hot, and you could get burned."

A few minutes later, you reach for a cookie that's on the pan, but then you remember what your mom said. You decide to not touch the pan and wait for her to come help.

God wants you to learn from people who know what is best for you. That's important, but it's even more important to listen to Him. God always knows what is best for you.

Lord, thank You that You and others teach me. Help me act on what I learn.

God teaches me what to do!

God Is Always Near

*You are all around me—in front and in back. You
have put your hand on me.*

—PSALM 139:5

Did you know that God is always near and
always taking care of you?

Mom and Dad take care of you too, but they don't
go to school or to a friend's house with you. But God
is always with you, even at school and playdates.

God is always willing to help you know what is
best and make good decisions. God is always able to
remind you that He loves you when you feel sad. And
God can always help you feel
better when you have a bad day.
God loves you, and He is
always taking care of you.

*Dear Lord, thank You for always
loving me and taking care of me.*

God is near and
takes care of me.

Sing to the Lord!

Skies, sing for joy because the Lord did great things! . . . Sing, too, you trees in the forest!
—ISAIAH 44:23

God has done a lot of great things, hasn't He? He created the world and all the people and animals and plants and mountains and everything else on it! The earth shows how great God is, and we can sing for joy because of the wonderful things He has done.

God planned for families, and He gave you parents and grandparents and cousins and aunts and uncles. Families are pretty great!

God also gave us Jesus, and God forgives our sins. Those are other great things that God has done.

What great things are you glad God did? Take a second to sing a song about how great you think He is!

Dear God, thank You for all of the great things you have done!

I will sing about the great things God has done!

Dr. Patrick Latham, First Baptist Church Lawton, Lawton, OK   131

God Gives Us All We Need

God said, "Look, I have given you all the plants that have grain for seeds. And I have given you all the trees whose fruits have seeds in them. They will be food for you."
—GENESIS 1:29

Have you ever watched birds flying around or sitting in trees? Have you ever watched them search for food on the ground and wondered if they would find anything to eat? Did you know that God takes care of birds? When God created the world, He made food for the birds just like He made food for you.

God loves you very much, and He makes sure that you have everything that you need.

Take some time now to thank God for giving you everything you need.

Dear Lord, thank You for taking really good care of me every day.

I know that God will give me all I need.

Dr. Patrick Latham, First Baptist Church Lawton, Lawton, OK

God Is Good

"No one is good except God alone."
—MARK 10:18

G od never does anything wrong. He never messes up like we do. We sometimes do things we know we shouldn't do. Sometimes we *don't* do what we know we *should* do. Only God is always perfectly good.

Whenever we do something wrong, we need to tell God that we are sorry. He will forgive us and help us do better.

God knows you can never be perfect. He helps you to be good. And He still loves you when you mess up. He will always love you.

Good and perfect God, thank You for helping me be good like You are.

God is always good.

God, the One and Only

There is no one like the God of Israel. . . . He rides
on the clouds in his majesty.
—DEUTERONOMY 33:26

Have you ever flown in an airplane? If you have, you know that when the plane is high up in the sky, you can look down and see everything—and everything looks different!

God looks at all the world and at your life—kind of like when we look down on highways and houses from an airplane. Your life looks different to God than it does to you. God sees everything, and He knows everything about all that He sees. No one else can know what God knows!

How powerful and wonderful and amazing is God!

God, You are the One and only God, and I praise You!

There is no one like God.

God's Helpers

*"I tell you that [children] have angels in heaven
who are always with my Father in heaven."*
—MATTHEW 18:10

A helper is someone who works with others to make their lives a little easier. Did you know that God has helpers? He has special helpers called *angels.* We don't know a lot about angels, but we know they live with God in heaven. We know that sometimes God sends an angel to earth with a special message. At other times, angels protect God's people.

God knows how important it is for us to have help when we need it. That's why He sends angels.

Even though we cannot see angels, we know that God will send them to help us when we need help.

Dear God, thank You for sending angels to help me when I need help.

Angels are
God's helpers.

Gina Napier, Sugar Hill Church, Sugar Hill, GA

A Worker for Jesus

*"There are a great many people to harvest. But
there are only a few workers to harvest them."*
—LUKE 10:2

Have you ever seen or read about a farm?
There is always work to be done on a farm.
Farmers get up early and work hard all day. They
have animals to feed, seeds to plant, vegetables
to pick, eggs to gather, fields to plow, crops to
harvest, barns to keep clean—and the list goes on.
A farmer's work never ends.

Just like the farmer, we who love Jesus have a
job that never ends. That job is to tell people that
Jesus loves them and wants to be their Savior. Is
that something you can do? Absolutely!

*Jesus, please help me tell people that You
love them and to be a good worker for You.*

I can tell others
that Jesus
loves them!

Gina Napier, Sugar Hill Church, Sugar Hill, GA

A New Creation

The old things have gone; everything is made new!
—2 CORINTHIANS 5:17

Caterpillars don't stay caterpillars forever. God designed them to change into something very different. Caterpillars go through a special change, and they become beautiful butterflies! The old body that crawled on the ground goes away, and a new one that can fly forms. Caterpillars and butterflies are very, very different!

When we decide to love Jesus, we are changed too. Our bodies don't change. The change happens inside of us. God helps our hearts know Him better, love Him, and love people. It's a good and beautiful change—just like a caterpillar into a butterfly!

Dear God, please keep changing my heart so that I love You and others more.

Jesus makes us new!

God Cares for Us

You made the moon to mark the seasons. And the sun always knows when to set.

—Psalm 104:19

Have you noticed that the sun comes up every morning and it goes down every night? God makes that happen.

God gives us the light of the sun so we can play and work, but He also gives us the dark of night so we can rest.

God made days and nights for a reason. He knows exactly what we need and when we need it. He knows we need to rest, so He gives us nights to stop working and sleep. Sunrises and sunsets can remind us that God takes care of us.

God, thank You for making this world, for making me, and for taking care of me.

God cares for me!

Night Guard

He who guards you never sleeps.
—Psalm 121:3

A guard is someone who watches over people to make sure they are safe. A night guard watches over people at night. Are you afraid of the dark—especially when it's time to go to sleep at night? If so, you aren't the only one who doesn't like the dark.

But did you know that nighttime doesn't have to be scary? Not at all! And that's because you can trust God to take care of you even while you sleep. He is your night guard. When you go to sleep at night, God is still awake! God *never* sleeps, so He can protect you every minute you are asleep and every minute you are awake. That's good news! God watches over you.

Thank You, God, for protecting me when I sleep and when I am awake.

I can trust God to
keep me safe.

Tell the Truth

*A messenger you can trust is just as refreshing
as cool water in summer.*

—PROVERBS 25:13 CEV

Have you ever touched a hot slide in the summer? Ouch!

What makes you cool when it is really hot outside? Maybe you jump into a swimming pool. Or maybe you drink a big glass of water with lots of ice. The water feels so good, whether you are in it or you drink it!

It feels so good to tell the truth too. When you do not tell the truth, you feel bad inside, and God feels bad. Telling the truth is like cool water that everyone loves.

*God, please help me
always tell the truth like You do.*

God wants me
to always tell
the truth.

Kim Whitt, Abilene Baptist Church, Augusta, GA

I Am Special

God had special plans for me even before I was born.
—GALATIANS 1:15

Have you made special plans for your birthday? You might choose a chocolate cake. Maybe you will invite friends to come over to play.

God also makes plans. And He made a special plan for your life before you were born. He picked out your mom and your dad just for you. He chose the color of your eyes, the color of your hair, and everything else about you. God made you very special so that you can do a very special job for Him. As you grow up, God will show you the job He has planned for you.

Thank You, God, for loving me and making the very best plan for me.

God has special plans for me.

God Listens to Me

Lord, every morning you hear my voice. Every morning, I tell you what I need. And I wait for your answer.
—PSALM 5:3

Who is the first person you talk to every morning? Maybe you say, "Good morning, Mom! What's for breakfast?"

You can wake up every day and also say, "Good morning, God!" He will be glad to hear your voice. God likes you to talk to Him just like you talk to your mom and dad. You can ask Him to help your sick friend feel better. You can tell Him what you need, how you are feeling, and if you are worried about something, and He will hear you. God loves to hear your voice!

Father, thank You for hearing my prayers. Remind me to talk to You during the day.

I will talk to God every morning.

God Is Everywhere

If I rise with the sun in the east, and settle in the west beyond the sea, even there you would guide me.
—PSALM 139:9-10

D o you try to hide from people when you mess up? When you were little and you accidentally broke a vase, maybe you crawled under your bed and hoped Mom would not find you.

Well, you cannot hide from God when you mess up. God sees and hears everything you do. He always knows where you are—and God is always there to take care of you. He will help you make good choices.

Always remember that God is everywhere. Even if you go someplace new and strange, He is with you. He will never leave you!

Father, thank You for being with me, taking care of me, and helping me make good choices.

God is
everywhere.

Sharing Love

Do not forget to do good to others. And share with them
what you have. These are the sacrifices that please God.
—HEBREWS 13:16

I t can be hard to share. You never know what will happen to the things you share. Your brother might lose your new LEGOs. Your sister might color on your best doll. But since you love your brother and sister more than your toys, you still share.

God is very happy when we share and show people we love them. God shares a lot with us to show us He loves us. He shares this beautiful world He made! God also shares His love, His kindness, and His goodness with us. We can share those things too.

Lord, thank You for all You share with me.
Help me share with my friends.

I want to share
God's love
with others.

Kim Whitt, Abilene Baptist Church, Augusta, GA

God Is So Good

*With praise and thanksgiving, [God's people]
sang to the Lord: "He is good."*

—EZRA 3:11

What is your favorite song to sing? Do you sing it when you're happy or when you're sad? Music can make us happier. And songs we sing to God can make us very happy.

God loves it when we sing to Him. When we sing, we can tell God how great and good He is. We can sing "Thank You" to God for loving us, taking care of us, and answering our prayers.

Singing to God is one way we can praise Him, thank Him, and show Him that we love Him.

*Lord, You are so good to me.
Thank You for loving me. I love
You very much!*

I want to sing to
God more often!

Pick Me!

God called you and chose you to be his.
—2 PETER 1:10

"Pick me!" we shout when Coach is choosing teams for T-ball. And when the teacher is choosing a line leader, we hope she picks us. But sometimes we aren't chosen to be on a certain team or to lead the recess line.

The good news is that Jesus will always choose you. If you pray, "Pick me, Jesus," He will! He loves you very much. Whether you are a boy or girl, or big or little—and no matter how old you are—He wants you on His team. He will pick you!

Dear God, thank You for picking me to be on Your team.

God picked me!

Sharing Home

Open your homes to each other, without complaining.
—1 PETER 4:9

Joey loved going to Michael's house. For hours and hours they would play with their toys. Joey had racecars, and Michael had action figures. Sharing with each other made playing more fun.

Maybe your family is friends with another family, and you share in a lot of ways. You share when you go on vacations together, you share meals, you share prayer requests, and you share God's love.

God wants us to share everything we have— because God shares everything He has with us!

God, thank You for all You have given me. Please help me share with others.

God wants me to share without complaining.

The Greatest Love of All

Christ's love is greater than any person can ever know. But I pray that you will be able to know that love. Then you can be filled with the fullness of God.
—EPHESIANS 3:19

H ave you ever watched a mommy with her baby? The love in that mommy's heart is bigger than her child could ever understand.

And God loves you more than you can really understand. God loves you so much He let His Son, Jesus, die for you. You and I do bad things called *sins*. God is good, so He has to punish bad. But He let Jesus be punished for our sins instead of punishing us. So we try not to do any more bad things, but when we mess up, God will forgive us because He loves us.

Dear God, thank You that no matter what I do, You will always love me.

God's love is bigger than you can imagine!

Dr. Benny Tate, Rock Springs Church, Milner, GA

Put on Love Every Day

Love is what holds you all together in perfect unity.
—COLOSSIANS 3:14

Every morning we get up, and we put on our shirt, pants, socks, and shoes. But if we stop there, we are forgetting something very important. God wants us to also put on love.

"Put on love" is just a fancy way of saying that we decide to be nice to people, obey our parents, be good at school, share when we have a chance, tell the truth, and pray to God. When you put on God's love, people will see how God's love makes you special.

So every morning when you put on your clothes, remember to put on love too. You will make God smile.

Dear God, help me remember to put on love every day.

I want to put on love.

Plenty to Eat

You will have plenty to eat. You will be full. You will praise the name of the Lord your God.
—JOEL 2:26

Benny loved banana pudding and strawberry cake, but he didn't like green beans at all.

But you know what? Every time, before Benny started eating, he bowed his head and prayed. He thanked God for the food God had given him and his family.

God has made sure we have food to eat. Some we like, and some, not so much. But even when dinner includes something we don't like, let's thank God for giving us food to eat.

Before every meal, take a few minutes to pray and thank God for the food.

Dear God, thank You for feeding me. Because of You I am full and healthy.

I will thank God for the food I have.

Thank You, God!

[The priests'] relatives stood across from them.
They gave praise and thanksgiving to God.
—NEHEMIAH 12:24

Shelby's daddy loved to hear her say "Thank you" when he did something special for her. He liked knowing she was thankful for what he did, and he liked knowing that she felt loved by him.

Like Shelby's dad, God also likes to hear us say "Thank You" to Him. And we have a lot to thank Him for! Everything you have is from God. Everything!

So today, thank God for your parents, your home, all the stuff you have, and especially for Jesus.

God loves to hear you pray, and He especially loves hearing "Thank You!"

Dear God, thank You for sending Jesus to die for me. Thanks for loving me that much.

I will thank God for everything!

Dr. Benny Tate, Rock Springs Church, Milner, GA

Not Too Much!

If you find honey, don't eat too much. Too much of it will make you sick.

—PROVERBS 25:16

H ave you ever eaten too much candy and gotten an upset stomach? That can happen!

A long time ago, people used honey to make food sweet. God created honey for people to enjoy, but too much honey can mean we will feel yucky. God made the sun so we can be warm, but too much sun can mean a sunburn. God gave us friends to play with, but too much playing can mean not enough time for other important things.

God wants us to enjoy what He made for us—but not too much at one time!

God, thank You for all the good things You have given me to enjoy.

I want to enjoy all the good things God gives me.

Ben Hunley, Second Baptist Church, Warner Robins, GA

Hidden Treasure

*I pray that you will know that the blessings God has
promised his holy people are rich and glorious.*
—EPHESIANS 1:18

Wouldn't it be so cool to find hidden treasure!
Imagine lying down in all the gold coins
and making a "snow angel." Picture the sparkling
diamonds and rubies and sapphires. This treasure
would be great, but not anywhere near as great as
the treasures God gives us.

God lets us talk to Him. He gave us the Bible. He
let His Son, Jesus, die for our sins. God loves us.
He adopts us as His children. He
has a place for us in heaven. And
He has forgiven our sins. These
are the best treasures ever!

*Thank You, God, for all the
great things You give to
people who love You.*

Jesus is the best
treasure ever.

From Dirty to Clean

Create in me a pure heart, God. Make my spirit right again.
—PSALM 51:10

Have you ever played in the mud and gotten your clothes all dirty? Sometimes it can be really tough to get those clothes clean again.

When we disobey God, we are sinning. (Sin is doing something God does not want us to do or *not* doing something God tells us to do.) And just like mud makes clothes dirty, our sin makes our hearts dirty. Not the heart in our chests, but the part of us that loves God. God is the only One who can make our hearts clean again. And He will.

God, I don't want my heart to be dirty with sin. Please clean my heart.

God is the only One who can clean my heart!

Be Glad!

Be satisfied with what you have.
—HEBREWS 13:5

H ave you ever had a friend who got a really cool toy that you wanted?

It is easy to think about the things we want but do not have. But God does not want us to think about that! He wants us to think about the long list of things He has given us. Some we can touch— like family, friends, and food—and some we can't touch—like love and forgiveness.

God wants us to thank Him for the things He gives us. He knows we'll be happier when we do.

God, thank You for all that You give me. You love me so much!

I will be happy with the things God has given me.

Ben Hunley, Second Baptist Church, Warner Robins, GA

Trust and Obey

He gives a command to the earth, and it quickly obeys him.

—PSALM 147:15

It can be hard to obey God. Moses had a tough time obeying God sometimes. God told him to go to the very powerful king of Egypt, called the pharoah, and Moses was scared.

Like Moses, we can be afraid to obey God. We may be scared, for instance, because telling the truth might get us in trouble. Or we might be scared to try something new.

When God tells the earth what to do, it just does it! When God tells the wind to blow or the waves to crash, they do not ask any questions. They do what God says. We should obey God like that too.

God, please help me to obey You without feeling afraid or asking questions.

I want to obey God like the wind and the waves.

Ben Hunley, Second Baptist Church, Warner Robins, GA

In Control!

He spreads the snow like wool. He scatters the frost like ashes.
—PSALM 147:16

Maybe it snows where you live. Maybe you've only seen pictures of snow. Either way, think about how the ground looks when it is covered with snow. Everything is perfectly white and smooth and beautiful.

And God made it that way: He controls the snow—and the wind and frost and heat. He makes it rain, and He makes it dry. He makes it hot or cold. Our strong God is in control of the weather. He created the earth, and He makes everything work together.

God also created you, and He loves you!

Thank You, God, for creating everything. Thank You for creating me and for loving me.

God is in control.

God Is in Charge

No one can stand the cold he sends. Then he
gives a command, and it melts.

—PSALM 147:17–18

What is your favorite season? Is it winter, spring, summer, or fall? Whichever one it is, God created it. God created all the seasons!

Maybe winter is your favorite season because God sometimes sends snow. Have you ever built a snowman? If you have, you know it doesn't last forever. It melts away.

God is the Creator of everything, and He is in control of everything. He sends snow, and He melts snow. When He gives a command, all creation obeys Him. God's power is great. So are His goodness and His love. Let's praise Him!

Good and powerful God, I'm glad You are in control of the beautiful world You made.

The God I love
sends the seasons.

There Is No One like God

Are there any gods like you, Lord? No! There are
no gods like you. You are wonderfully holy. You
are amazingly powerful. You do great miracles.
—EXODUS 15:11

W hat is your name? It's crazy to think about, but someone else on this planet may have that same name. Even if a hundred people have your name, though, no one is exactly like you! There is only one you—and there is only one true God.

The God we read about in the Bible created us, He loves us, and He is powerful. He heals us and helps us. He guides us and comforts us. He is a wonderful and amazing God.

And God wants us to love Him more than we love anything or anyone else.

Dear God, You are so wonderful and powerful.
Help me love You with all my energy.

I love the only
true God.

Jill Baumgardner, Concord Baptist Church, Clermont, GA   159

Happy, Happy, Happy!

My child, if you are wise, then I will be happy.
—PROVERBS 23:15

Maybe you know the wise old owl from the stories of Winnie-the-Pooh. Owls are sometimes thought to be wise because they seem to do a lot of watching and listening. We aren't owls, but we can learn a lot by watching and listening too.

God also tells us that He gives us wisdom. That means God makes us able to understand what Jesus said in the Bible and then do it. We should always be learning about Jesus and doing what He said. When we do that, Jesus is very happy.

Dear Jesus, thank You for the Bible that tells me what You want me to do.

I want to live the way Jesus says.

Jill Baumgardner, Concord Baptist Church, Clermont, GA

Our God Rules

God is supreme over the skies. His greatness covers the earth.
—PSALM 57:5

When you play outside in the beautiful world God made, do you ever stop to look up at the very big sky above you? Maybe you see birds flying, clouds floating, or an airplane far away. That big sky covers the whole earth.

God created that very big sky, and He rules the sky just as He rules the whole earth. Our great God is lovelier than the bluest sky, He is more powerful than the thunder and lightning in a stormy sky, and He controls the sunrises and the sunsets. He is an awesome God!

Dear God, thank You for being the great and strong and mighty Ruler over everything.

God is Ruler over *everything.*

Sharing God's Love

Good people always lend freely to others.
—Psalm 37:26

Has anyone ever given you something for free? Maybe someone gave you a special toy that you had wanted for a long time. Maybe it was hard to share that new toy with your brother or sister or friend.

It is not always easy to share (especially something new)! But God wants us to share what we have. He wants us to think about other people and not just about ourselves. We show God's love when we share with people who don't have enough. And God is pleased when we share, especially His love.

God, help me to share with others what You have given me.

I want to share Jesus with others.

Step-by-Step

*When a man's steps follow the Lord, God is
pleased with his ways. If he stumbles, he will not
fall, because the Lord holds his hand.*
—PSALM 37:23–24

Have you ever watched babies learning to walk? They stand up and try to get their balance. Slowly, carefully, and sometimes holding someone's hand, the baby puts one foot forward. It's a big day when this little person takes steps without holding hands.

It's a big day for Jesus whenever we take steps in the direction He wants us to go. Jesus wants us to do what He tells us to do. When we obey, Jesus is happy. When we do not obey, we stumble, but Jesus does not let go of us. He is with us step-by-step as we follow Him.

Dear God, I want You to be pleased by how I live.

I want to make
Jesus happy!

Jill Baumgardner, Concord Baptist Church, Clermont, GA   163

We Are Never Alone

The Lord ... will not leave those who worship him.
He will always protect them.

—PSALM 37:28

D o you have a favorite toy or stuffed animal that you like to take wherever you go? Do you have a good friend or a fun cousin whom you like to do things with?

Well, you cannot always have a toy or a friend with you. But even when you can't take a toy or a friend, you are not alone. No matter where you go, God is with you. You can't see Him, but you can be sure He is taking good care of you. He promised to do that, and God always keeps His promises.

God, thank You for being with me and taking good care of me.

I am never alone because God is always with me!

Kelly Cathey, First Baptist Bossier, Bossier City, LA

I Will Be Fair

A good person speaks with wisdom. He says what is fair.
—PSALM 37:30

"That's not fair!" We have all said that before, haven't we? When something is not fair, we feel sad and even angry. We want everyone to be treated the same way. If you get a cookie and your brother does too, that is fair. It is not fair if only one of you gets a cookie!

God wants us to be fair. We are fair when we are kind to everyone, not just to certain people. We are fair when we treat people equally.

Find ways to be fair. Being kind shows people God's love.

Dear God, please help me be kind and fair today and every day.

I want to be kind and fair to everyone.

God Will Help

Wait for the Lord's help and follow him.
—Psalm 37:34

We all wait. We wait in line at the movies. We wait for dinner to be ready. We wait for Christmas so we can open the gifts under the tree.

The most important thing we can wait for is God's help. When we ask God to help us, He will. He will help us be patient. He will help us share. And He will help us make decisions.

Then, when God helps us make decisions, we do what He wants us to do—and He continues to help us.

God, thank You for helping me make decisions every day.

I will wait for God's help and follow Him.

Being More like God

It is good to be kind and generous.
—Psalm 112:5

Think about all the good things that you have. Every single good thing you have is a gift from God. And God gives you and me so many good things because He loves us.

Whenever we are kind and whenever we share with people, we are treating them in the same way God treats us. So today be kind to people because God is kind to you. And be generous because God is generous to you. Think about all the things that you can share. For starters, you can share big hugs, high fives, and awesome smiles.

God, thank You for being kind and generous to me. Help me be kind and generous.

I want to be kind and generous like God is to me!

Kelly Cathey, First Baptist Bossier, Bossier City, LA

God Is Not Mad at Me

The Lord says, "I will forgive them for leaving me. I will love them freely. I am not angry with them anymore."
—HOSEA 14:4

Maybe we didn't share our toys or we said mean words to a friend. Maybe we didn't tell the truth or we hurt someone's feelings.

We all do wrong things and make bad choices, and we are sad after we do them. When we mess up, though, we can pray and ask God to forgive us. God is glad that we understand we messed up (that's called *sin*), He is pleased when we tell Him about those bad things (that's called *confessing*), and He loves to forgive us!

God is happy that we want to be good.

God, thank You for not being mad at me and for loving me so much.

Jesus will forgive me when I ask.

Kelly Cathey, First Baptist Bossier, Bossier City, LA

Jesus Will Take Care of Me

[A good person] is safe because he trusts the Lord.
—PSALM 112:7

We trust all kinds of things. We trust the roof of our houses to keep us dry when it rains. We trust a chair to hold us up when we sit on it. We trust friends to keep secrets that we tell them.

But Jesus is the only One who will never let us down. Our roof could leak, our chair could break, and friends could tell other people our secrets. But Jesus will never disappoint us. We can trust that Jesus will always take care of us and keep us safe.

Jesus, thank You that I can trust You to always keep me safe!

I trust Jesus to take care of me.

Never Alone

*"I will walk with you and be your God. And you
will be my people."*

—LEVITICUS 26:12

D o you like taking walks with a friend? Those
can be fun adventures. As you walk, you can
talk about things you see, how you are feeling, or
what you are thinking. Or the two of you can just
enjoy being with each other.

Did you know that God wants to walk with you?
Walking with God means spending time with
Him by praying and reading His Word. It means
talking to God about what is happening in your life
and how you are feeling. Or you
can just enjoy knowing God is
walking with you.

*Dear God, I love You. Help me
walk close to You every day.*

God walks with me.

A Special Name

A child will be born to us. God will give a son to us. He will be responsible for leading the people. His name will be Wonderful Counselor, Powerful God.

—ISAIAH 9:6

Some of us don't have a middle name. Some of us have a crazy nickname. All of us have a name that is special. Our names are special because they give others a way to know who we are.

Like your name, Jesus' name helps us know who He is. Actually, Jesus has many names, and they all tell us something about Him. The name *Wonderful Counselor* tells us Jesus is marvelous and teaches us how to follow God. His name *Powerful God* tells us Jesus is God, not just a man. Jesus is a name greater than any other.

Dear God, thank You for the gift of Jesus, my Wonderful Counselor and Powerful God.

I can know more about Jesus through His names.

Analisa Hood and Suzanne Walker,
Mobberly Baptist Church, Longview, TX

God Is Great!

Show your servants the wonderful things you do.
Show your greatness to their children.

—PSALM 90:16

Would you like to see God? When we are in heaven, we will see God, but until we go to heaven, we can know God through the words in our Bibles and the great things He does.

God's greatness is everywhere. God's greatness is in the warmth of the golden sun and in the sparkling stars across the night sky. God's greatness is in the rocky cliffs of the biggest mountain and in the tiny hand of a newborn baby.

God's greatness shows up most clearly in His great love: He let His Son, Jesus, take the punishment for our sins.

Dear God, I praise You for Your greatness and for Your great love for me.

I love a very great and very wonderful God!

Analisa Hood and Suzanne Walker,
Mobberly Baptist Church, Longview, TX

Tender Loving Care

*The Lord has mercy on those who fear him, as a
father has mercy on his children.*
—PSALM 103:13

Have you ever held a kitten and stroked its soft fur? You were gentle. You showed kindness to the baby animal.

The mighty God who created the universe and controls the sea is also very gentle and very kind. He shows His care for people who love Him in many ways. God shows He cares by creating the beautiful world around you, by making the rain fall and watering the earth, and by giving us family and friends to spend time with. Those are a few ways that God shows His tender loving care.

*Dear God, help me show
kindness with the words I say
and the things I do.*

I can be kind like
God is kind to me.

Love, Love, Love

*The Lord shows mercy and is kind. He does not
become angry quickly, and he has great love.*
—Psalm 103:8

A list of words describing our amazing God
would be a very, very long list. And every
word on that list would be something good!

Let's start a list: God is kind and understanding.
God is slow to get angry with people because
He loves us a lot. In fact, the word on the list that
would be written the biggest and the boldest is
LOVE. God's love is the absolutely most important
thing about Him. God wants you
to know Him and His great
love for you.

*God, teach me more about
Your great love for me, and help
me share it with others.*

The greatest
thing about God
is His love.

Don't Forget to Remember

Remember Jesus Christ.
—2 TIMOTHY 2:8

Is it good to think of Jesus when you are eating breakfast or learning math at school? When you are happy and excited, or when you are lonely or tired? When everything is going just right, or when everything is wrong?

The answer is yes to all of the above—think of Jesus at all these times and in all these places! It is always right to think about Jesus and His love for you. It is always good to remember Jesus is with you in whatever way you need Him.

So, don't forget to remember Jesus!

God, please help me think about Jesus every hour of every day.

I don't want
to forget to
remember Jesus.

Analisa Hood and Suzanne Walker,
Mobberly Baptist Church, Longview, TX

Give Thanks to God

*Give thanks to the God of heaven. His love
continues forever.*

—PSALM 136:26

Who are some of the people you love? Mom, Dad, your sister, or brother? Your grandparents? Friends? Your Sunday school teacher? Your babysitter?

We love many people in our lives, and many people in our lives love us a lot. But God loves us even more than any one of them does. God loves us far more than we can imagine.

It is good to thank God every day for His love and for many other blessings He gives us. What three blessings will you thank God for right now?

Dear God, thank You for loving me and giving me so many blessings.

I am thankful for God's love and many blessings.

Chris Bridges, Calvary Church, Clearwater, FL

Obedience Pleases God

"So now obey me.... Do this, and you will be my
own possession, chosen from all the nations."
—EXODUS 19:5

You may feel that you have to obey a lot of people. You obey Mom, Dad, teachers, and coaches. And all of us need to obey police officers, follow safety rules, and follow our country's laws.

God, however, is the most important One who all of us should obey. And God wants us to obey Him in all we do, all we say, and all we think. The good news is that God will help us obey Him—and then He is pleased when we do obey Him.

Dear God, help me obey the people I need to obey— and help me obey You!

I will obey God with my thoughts, words, and actions.

Anywhere and Everywhere

Surely the Lord is in this place. But I did not know it.
—GENESIS 28:16

Have you ever seen the wind? Can you see the air you breathe? No one has ever seen the wind or the air!

We can feel the cool breeze and see the leaves blowing. Still, we cannot actually see the wind even when it blows all around us.

Just like we can't see the wind, we cannot see God. But just like the air we breathe, He is all around us. God is with us all the time, wherever we go. There is no place that we can go and be away from God.

Dear God, thank You for always being with me anywhere and everywhere I go.

I am happy that God is with me wherever I go.

God's Good Care

"I tell you, don't worry about the food you need to live. Don't worry about the clothes you need for your body."
—LUKE 12:22

What are some things you think about a lot? Maybe you often think about what to wear or what to eat. There are a lot of things in life that we can think about a lot, and sometimes we begin to worry about them.

Jesus told us not to worry. He also told us to think about God. You can think about His love, His goodness, His generosity, His patience, His kindness, and His faithfulness. And when you think about God, you will remember that He always takes good care of you.

Dear God, please help me to focus on You instead of worrying about things.

I will not worry because God will take care of me.

Gifts for Jesus

After Jesus was born, some wise men from the east came to Jerusalem.

—MATTHEW 2:1

After Jesus was born, wise men traveled a long way to see this young King and to worship Him. The wise men took Jesus gifts of gold, spices, and perfume. These valuable gifts showed Jesus that the wise men honored Him and loved Him.

We honor Jesus when we act in a way that shows we think He is important. What can you do to honor Jesus? Spend time with Him by praying and reading the Bible. Be kind to people. Always tell the truth. Talk to people about Jesus.

Honoring Jesus is a good gift to give Him.

Dear God, please help me be like the wise men and show Jesus honor and love.

I will honor Jesus and love Him all my life.

Chris Bridges, Calvary Church, Clearwater, FL

Serve the Lord

Serve the Lord with joy. Come before him with singing.
—PSALM 100:2

Did you know you can serve the Lord by helping around your house? It's true! You don't have to be a pastor to serve Jesus.

Think about the jobs you have at home. When you do your chores at home, you are serving your family, and that makes God happy. What makes God even happier is when you serve your family with joy! At dinner tonight, talk about how each of you can serve God and how you as a family can serve Him.

Remember: when we serve with joy, we are being obedient to God.

Dear God, whatever You want me to do, please help me serve You with joy.

I will serve the
Lord with joy.

The Lord Is Good

The Lord is good. His love continues forever. His loyalty continues from now on.

—Psalm 100:5

T hings we call good often make us happy. Good friends, good food, and good grades make us smile.

But God is good in a much bigger way! He is the Giver of everything good, and He is the best example of how to be good. God keeps His promises, He never lies, and He can always be trusted. God is wise, He is patient, and His love will last forever. God is truly good!

Lord, thank You for being a good God who loves me and takes care of me.

The Lord is good.

An Act of Worship

*[The wise men] bowed down and worshiped the
child. They opened the gifts they brought for him.*
—MATTHEW 2:11

T he star the wise men saw was different from
any star they had ever seen. But they knew
from their studies that a special star would show
them when a special king was born. So the wise men
followed the star to Jesus. The wise men understood
who Jesus was. Do you know who Jesus is?

The wise men knew that God had promised to
send Jesus, the special King of the Jewish people—
and of everyone else who would love and serve Him.

So the wise men worshiped the young King. They
gave Him honor and gifts. We should also honor
Jesus, love Him, and serve Him.

*Dear God, help me worship You and
follow Jesus in ways that honor You both.*

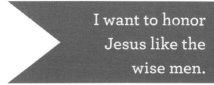

I want to honor
Jesus like the
wise men.

God's Assignment

The angel came to [Mary] and said, "Greetings!
The Lord has blessed you and is with you."
—LUKE 1:28

The Lord sent the angel Gabriel to Mary with this very important message: God had chosen Mary to be the mother of His Son.

Of course Mary didn't expect an angel to visit. She was surprised.

Gabriel told Mary that God had blessed her by choosing her to be Jesus' mother. That was a huge assignment! But what was Mary's response? "I am the Lord's servant, and I am willing to do whatever He wants me to do."

May you say that when Jesus gives you an assignment!

Jesus, help me know when You want me to do something—and help me do it.

I want to say yes to anything God asks.

Dr. Rob Zinn, Immanuel Baptist Church, Highland, CA

As He Always Did

Jesus traveled to Nazareth, where he had grown up. On the Sabbath day he went to the synagogue as he always did.
—LUKE 4:16

Pay attention to those last four words in today's Bible verse: *as he always did.*

The synagogue is where Jesus worshipped. It was Jesus' church. And Jesus always went to church, whether He was in His hometown or traveling. Church was a built-in part of Jesus' life.

Since God loves us and calls us His children, we should want to go to church. We should not have to decide every week whether or not we want to go. We should go because we love God and because He wants us to be with His people worshipping, praying, and learning the Bible.

Jesus, please give me a heart that wants to worship You and learn the Bible.

I want go to church like Jesus.

The Light of the World

"I am the light of the world. The person who follows me will never live in darkness."

—JOHN 8:12

In the Bible, Jesus gave Himself several names to help us know Him better. One time Jesus said that He was "the light of the world."

But Jesus is not a light for us to look at the way we look at a traffic light. Jesus is a light that helps us see ahead and move forward. Just as we need a flashlight in the dark, and Mom needs headlights to drive at night, Jesus gives us light to help us go where He wants us to go and do what He wants us to do.

Jesus, help me to follow You by walking in the light You give me!

Jesus is the light of the world.

God Keeps His Promises

This is what the Lord says: I have an agreement with day and night. . . . Day and night will always come at the right times.
—JEREMIAH 33:20

God keeps His promises! One promise He made is that there will always be day and night, and, as you can see, that's very true. When God makes a promise, you can trust Him to keep it.

God has already kept many promises He made in the Bible. God promised to send His Son, Jesus— and we celebrate Christmas because God kept that promise. God promised that Jesus would be the winner over death and sin—and we celebrate Easter because Jesus did not stay dead!

Let every morning and every night help you remember that God keeps His promises.

Dear God, thank You for making wonderful promises and for keeping them.

I need to keep my promises.

Dr. Rob Zinn, Immanuel Baptist Church, Highland, CA

Our Never-Changing God

"I am the Lord. I do not change."
—MALACHI 3:6

It is great news that God never changes! That truth means God will always be powerful and good and merciful and kind and wise and patient and in charge of everything. He will always be King of kings, our good Shepherd, and our everlasting heavenly Father. God will always keep His promises.

And He will always love you. There is not one thing you could do or say that would change God's love for you. He has chosen to love you, and our never-changing God will never change His mind.

Thank You, Lord, that You love me and that You will always love me.

God never changes.

Mrs. Mary Cox,
North Metro First Baptist Church, Lawrenceville, GA

Being at Home with God

Lord, you have been our home since the beginning.
—PSALM 90:1

Have you lived in one house all your life? If so, that is a special blessing. You have shared good family times and special occasions in that house.

Have you lived in more than one house? That is a different kind of special blessing. You and your family have explored new places and made new friends.

The most important home you can have is God. He doesn't have windows or a garage like a house does, but He gives you peace and protection and a place to belong. What a blessing!

Dear God, thank You for loving me and giving me a forever home with You!

Thank You God for being my home.

Serving with All Your Heart

You must honor the Lord. You must always serve him with all your heart. Remember the wonderful things he did for you!
—1 SAMUEL 12:24

God has done wonderful things for you. He has shown His love for you by sending Jesus to be punished for your sins. God has given you family and friends and many more blessings.

You thank Him for these many blessings when you serve Him with all your heart. That means serving Him with all the love in your heart, with all the energy you can find, and with all the joy that He gives you.

And if you seem low on love, energy, and joy, ask God to give those to you. He will!

Thank you, God, for all the wonderful things You have done for me!

I want to serve God with all my heart.

Obeying the Rules

Why do you follow rules like these: "Don't handle this," "Don't taste that," "Don't touch that thing"?
—COLOSSIANS 2:20–21

Following the rules God gave us in the Bible is a very good thing. But we must not think more about the rules than about Jesus. In the Bible, we can read about people who loved rules so much that they made up a bunch of them for everyone else to follow. The rules quickly became more important than loving God!

When you love someone very much, obeying that person makes your heart happy. The more you love Jesus, the more you will obey Him. That's why loving Him is the very best thing you can do.

Lord, thank You for teaching me not just to obey but also to love You with all my heart.

I want to obey Jesus because I love Him.

Mrs. Mary Cox,
North Metro First Baptist Church, Lawrenceville, GA

Thinking About Others

Be humble and give more honor to others than to yourselves.
—PHILIPPIANS 2:3

When you get together with a friend, who usually talks first?

When you are quiet and let your friends talk first, you are showing them that they are important to you and that you are interested in what they have to say.

Next time you are with a friend, let your friend talk first, and you listen carefully. That is one way to be a good friend. And letting your friend talk first makes God happy. He likes when you make the other person more important than yourself.

God is always pleased when you think of others!

God, help me think about others first and help me listen more than I talk!

I want to listen more and think of others first.

Mrs. Mary Cox,
North Metro First Baptist Church, Lawrenceville, GA

Being a Servant

He was born as a man and became like a servant.
—PHILIPPIANS 2:7

When Jesus lived on the earth, He taught us how to be servants by being one Himself.

One day Jesus washed the feet of twelve friends just like a servant would have done. That was one way Jesus served. Jesus took our punishment and died on the cross. That was another big way He served people!

You don't have to wash feet or die on a cross to be a servant. What will you do to help someone in your family, a friend, or a neighbor?

When you serve, you are loving people.

Dear God, help me be a servant like Jesus! Give me someone to love and serve today.

I want to be like Jesus and serve others.

A Pure Heart

"Those who are pure in their thinking are happy.
They will be with God."

—MATTHEW 5:8

We like things that are clean and pure. We like clean clothes, clean cars, clean fruit, and clean bodies. We wash our hands, take baths, and brush our teeth in order to get clean. Mom likes us to be clean—even behind our ears.

God also likes for us to be clean—He uses the word *pure.* God especially likes clean and pure hearts. It takes soap and water to clean our bodies, but that's not how we clean our hearts. Instead, when we believe Jesus died for our sins, God sees our hearts as clean and pure.

✧ *Thank You, Father, for Your plan that gives me a clean and pure heart.* ✧

I can have
a clean heart!

A Sick Soul

"Healthy people don't need a doctor. It is the sick who need a doctor."

—LUKE 5:31

One day Clay became sick with an earache that hurt so bad it made him cry, so his mom took him to the doctor. Soon, Clay felt much better.

Our bodies get sick sometimes, but did you know that our hearts and souls can get sick too? Some people have a sick soul. That happens when we do things God doesn't want us to do. Who will help these people feel better?

Jesus will. He came to earth to heal everyone who has a sick soul—and all of us have a sick soul until we know Jesus' love. Let's help people meet Jesus so their souls can be healed.

Father, thank You that Jesus can heal everyone who has a sick soul.

Jesus heals the soul.

Dr. Clayton Cloer, Church at the Cross, Orlando, FL

When People Are Mean

"Those who are treated badly for doing good are happy. The kingdom of heaven belongs to them."
—MATTHEW 5:10

People were mean to Jesus. They made fun of Him. They spat on Him. They arrested Him when He had not done anything wrong. They even nailed Jesus to a cross.

But even when people were mean, Jesus was never mean to them. Even when Jesus was hanging on the cross, He asked God to forgive the people who were hurting Him. Jesus knew that those mean people did not know they were hurting the Son of God.

It's hard not to be mean when people are mean to us, but God can help us.

Dear God, help me not be mean when people are mean to me.

I know God will help me be kind.

Dr. Clayton Cloer, Church at the Cross, Orlando, FL

Knowing God

"They don't know the One who sent me."
—JOHN 15:21

We are blessed to know Jesus and God, His Father.

Jesus met people who knew *about* God, but they didn't know God well enough to see that Jesus was His Son.

It is sad that some people do not know Jesus. We can tell our friends about Jesus so that they can know that Jesus is God's Son and that He can save them too.

Father, give me the courage to tell my friends about Jesus so they can know You.

I can tell others about Jesus, God's Son.

How to Have Fruit

The Spirit gives love, joy, peace, patience, kindness, goodness, faithfulness, gentleness, self-control.
—GALATIANS 5:22–23

Apple trees grow apples. Orange trees grow oranges. Lemon trees grow lemons. But you already knew that! Did you know that when you love Jesus and follow Him, good things grow in your life?

What are these good things? They are gifts (also called fruit) from the Holy Spirit: love, joy, peace, patience, kindness, goodness, faithfulness, gentleness, and self-control. When you see this fruit in your life, you can know that you are living the way God wants you to live.

Holy Spirit, thank You for growing love, joy, kindness, and patience in my life.

The Holy Spirit grows good things in my life.

Hearing or Listening?

The Lord is trying to teach the people a lesson. He is
trying to make them understand his teachings.
—ISAIAH 28:9

D o you know the difference between hearing and listening? Hearing is being aware of noises and sounds and voices. Listening, though, is paying attention to what the noises are, what the sounds mean, and what the voices are saying and teaching.

Sometimes when we hear teachers or our parents talking, we know they are talking to us, but we don't pay attention to what they are saying. That's not good. And it's especially not good when we don't pay attention to what God is saying. It's important to listen to God's Word and obey.

Dear God, I want to listen to, understand, and obey Your teachings. Please help me.

I want to listen to
and understand
God's Word.

Dr. Clayton Cloer, Church at the Cross, Orlando, FL   199

Good Fruit

"If you want good fruit, you must make the tree good. If your tree is not good, then it will have bad fruit. A tree is known by the kind of fruit it produces."

—MATTHEW 12:33

What is your favorite fruit? Do you know how it grows? Some fruit grows on trees, like bananas; some on vines, like grapes; and some on plants, like strawberries. Fruit is good when the tree, vine, or plant it grows on is healthy.

Jesus helps us to do nice things for other people when He lives in our hearts. All the nice things we do are like yummy fruit. Just like healthy banana trees have bananas on their branches, you will have kind words, serve well, and be blessed when you love Jesus.

God, please help me to do nice things for others so I can be like yummy fruit.

> I want to have a healthy life with good fruit.

Dr. Don Wilton, First Baptist Church, Spartanburg, SC

Cuddly Love

Love, then, is what you should try for.
—1 CORINTHIANS 14:1

D o you have a soft blanket or teddy bear that you just love to cuddle with? Does that cuddling make you feel warm and safe?

Loving Jesus can make you feel even warmer and safer. Jesus loves you very much, and He wants you to cuddle up with Him by reading about Him in the Bible, praying to Him, and singing songs about Him.

When you cuddle up with Jesus, He helps you share that same cuddly love with your family and friends. Sharing that love makes Jesus happy.

God, thank You that when I read the Bible, pray, or sing, I feel Your warm love.

Jesus makes me
feel warm and safe.

Clean Hearts

Christ died for us while we were still sinners. In this way God shows his great love for us.
—ROMANS 5:8

On summer days Trevor loved to play outside, and he always got very dirty. When that happened, his mom would clean him up in the bathtub. Has this ever happened to you?

There's another way that we all have gotten really dirty. The dirt is sin. When we sin—when we don't do what Jesus wants us to do—we get really dirty with dirt that Jesus sees.

Jesus can forgive our sin and make our hearts clean when we ask Him to.

God, thank You that Jesus took my punishment for sin so I can be clean.

Jesus cleans my heart.

Following Jesus

*It always gives me the greatest joy when I hear
that my children are following the way of truth.*
—3 JOHN V. 4

O ne of Jesus' friends was the apostle John. John taught people about living in a way that would make Jesus happy. John called it "following the way of truth." Whenever John heard that people were following the truth, John was very happy.

Have you ever played Follow the Leader? You can follow your friends around the house and have fun. God loves when we follow Him. He wants us to follow Him everywhere. This makes Him very happy, and it is the best fun!

*Dear God, help me to follow Jesus
everywhere and every day.*

I will follow Jesus.

Patience and Trust

*Patient people have great understanding, but
people with quick tempers show their foolishness.*
—PROVERBS 14:29 NCV

It's so hard to wait for dinner to be ready when you are very, very hungry! It's hard to wait for your turn playing a game. And it's hard to wait for God to answer our prayers.

We all need to learn to wait, and that means learning to be patient. It's hard to be patient while you wait for God to answer prayers. But being patient is choosing to trust that God is doing good things in your life at the perfect time.

God knows what is best for you, and you can trust Him.

*Dear God, please help me learn to be
patient. I want to trust You more.*

**God can help me
be patient.**

Dr. Don Wilton, First Baptist Church, Spartanburg, SC

Praying for Grown-ups

Pray for the leaders so that we can have quiet and peaceful lives—lives full of worship and respect for God.
—1 TIMOTHY 2:2

There are lots of grown-ups all around you. Who are some of the important grown-ups in your life? I am sure you thought of Mommy or Daddy right away. And maybe you thought of your grandparents and your Sunday school teacher.

Did you think of the grown-ups who make decisions for your city, your state, and the country? God tells us to pray for these people so they will make good decisions that let us have "quiet and peaceful lives." When we pray for these leaders, we please and honor God.

God, thank You for answering when I pray for the grown-ups who are our leaders.

God answers my prayers.

My Gift to God

To your service for God, add kindness for your brothers
and sisters in Christ; and to this kindness, add love.
—2 PETER 1:7

D id you know you could give a gift to God? You can give God your service. What is service? When you serve someone, you help him or her. Isn't that amazing? God is all-powerful, but He still wants our help. God wants us to help Him by helping others. We help others by showing love and kindness. You can do this every day. You can share, use kind words, and take turns with your friends. Ask God to help you serve Him by showing love and kindness today.

Dear Jesus, help me serve You today by loving others and by being kind.

I will be kind and loving.

Better Than a Birthday Present

Grace and peace be given to you more and more.
You will have grace and peace because you truly
know God and Jesus our Lord.

—2 PETER 1:2

D o you remember the last time someone gave you a birthday present? When you know Jesus and He lives in your heart, He gives you two wonderful presents that are better than any birthday present. One is grace and the other is peace. Grace means God forgives us even when we don't deserve it. When we make mistakes, God will forgive us when we ask Him. Peace means we can have a calm and quiet heart. God helps our hearts feel safe even when we are scared. God gives great gifts.

Dear God, thank You for giving me great gifts.

God's greatest
gift is Jesus.

Paul and Kimberly Purvis,
First Baptist Church Temple Terrace, Temple Terrace, FL

Give God Your Best

Let goodness flow like a never-ending stream.
—AMOS 5:24

What is the best thing that's ever happened to you? What if that good thing kept happening over and over again? Since God gives us good things, He wants us to do good things for others. And guess what? He wants us to do them over and over again.

We can give God our best when we make good choices. Can you make good choices? Sure you can! Every day we have the chance to make good or bad choices. God will help us know how to make the best choice. When we make the best choices, we give God our all. God wants our goodness to "flow like a never-ending stream."

Dear God, thank You for giving me Your best. Help me to make good choices for You today.

Do something
good for
God today.

Paul and Kimberly Purvis,
First Baptist Church Temple Terrace, Temple Terrace, FL

Have Faith

"If your faith is not strong, then you will not have strength to last."

—ISAIAH 7:9

D o you want your heart to be strong? If so, you need to have faith. Faith means that you trust Jesus with all your heart. When you trust Jesus, God makes you strong enough to face anything in life.

We can trust Jesus to love us, take care of us, and always be with us. We can have faith in Him completely. God wants you to trust Him for everything with your whole heart. When we trust God, He makes our hearts and souls strong enough to face anything in life. The more we trust God, the stronger our faith and our hearts will grow.

Dear Jesus, I trust You. I know You love me. Thank You for making me strong!

I will have faith in God and be strong today.

Give the Gift of Kindness

*Let all men see that you are gentle and kind. The
Lord is coming soon.*

—PHILIPPIANS 4:5

It is very important that we show people how much God loves them. God showed us kindness by giving us Jesus. We can show God's love by being kind to people. There are many ways to be kind. We can do nice things for people. We can say hello and use loving words to everyone we see. We can even show kindness by smiling. When we are kind, others see God's love in us. This makes God's heart happy.

Dear Jesus, thank You for loving me. Help me to love others by being kind today.

It's always
right to be kind.

Spirit of Power

[God] gave us a spirit of power and love and self-control.

—2 TIMOTHY 1:7

T his week we have talked about some of the special gifts God gives us. We have also talked about special gifts we can give to others. Sometimes, when we think about what God wants us to do, it might seem hard to do. But the Bible says nothing is too hard for God. He will give you the power to do what you need to do. He will give you the power to love those who need love. And God will help you to be a good person. Keep trusting God. He'll give you all you need.

Thank You, God, for giving me Your Spirit of power.

God will help me.

Paul and Kimberly Purvis,
First Baptist Church Temple Terrace, Temple Terrace, FL

Our Amazing God

Come and see what God has done. See what
amazing things he has done for people.
—PSALM 66:5

God does amazing things. One time God made
a path of dry land through the sea so that
His people could get away from the Egyptians.
Jesus fed thousands of people with a couple of fish
and some bread. And the Holy Spirit made Jesus'
scared friends into bold teachers.

God still does amazing things. He tells the sun to
rise every morning. At night He lets the moon and
stars shine.

And even with all the people in the world, God
knows your name, and He loves you. Amazing, isn't
it? And very wonderful!

Dear God, not only are You powerful and good
and wise, but You are also truly amazing.

I want to see the
amazing things
God has done!

212   Missy Benfield, Prospect Baptist Church, Albemarle, NC

God Hears

God has listened. He has heard my prayer.
—Psalm 66:19

D id you know that God always hears you? Whenever you pray—from wherever you are—God hears your prayers. It doesn't matter where you are or what time it is. God is always listening.

He loves to hear you talk to Him. You don't need fancy words. You can talk to God like you talk to your best friend. Tell Him what you are thinking and feeling. He hears you every time you talk to Him. Spend some time talking with Him today and every day. You—and He—will be glad you did.

Dear God, thank You for hearing me whenever I pray. Help me remember to pray every day.

God hears my prayers.

Look at What God Can Do!

Stop and notice God's miracles.
—JOB 37:14

D o you know what a miracle is? It is something that only God can do.

The Bible talks about the miracles Jesus did. He walked on water. He told the winds and waves to stop, and they obeyed. He made blind people see and crippled people walk. But the greatest miracle of all is that Jesus rose from the dead!

Every day is filled with miracles too. Every baby born is a miracle. It's a miracle that birds fly. Your brain thinks, remembers, and dreams—and that's a miracle. Keep your eyes open for things only God can do!

Dear Jesus, help me to see Your miracles every day and praise You for them.

I want to see God's miracles.

God's Puzzling Name

God said to Moses, "I AM WHO I AM."
—Exodus 3:14

When God chose Moses to lead His people, Moses was afraid. Moses worried that the people would not believe that God had chosen him to be their leader.

So Moses asked God, "Who do I say sent me?" God told Moses to say, "I AM sent me." But what did that puzzling name mean?

By calling Himself "I AM," God was saying that He does exist, He is real, and He will always be the same. God will always be kind. He will never use up all His kindness. And He will never use up His patience, joy, kindness, and faithfulness. His love is everlasting.

Dear God, thank You for never changing. That makes it easier to know You and trust You.

God is the great I AM.

Missy Benfield, Prospect Baptist Church, Albemarle, NC

Watching over You

The Lord looks down from heaven. He sees every person.
—PSALM 33:13

D id you know God watches over you?

God sees every person in all the world, all at the same time. Yet He doesn't see all of us just as a big group. Because He is God, He can see each one-of-a-kind person in the group. So He knows your laugh and loves to hear it. He always hears you when you pray. He knows when you cry, and He knows when you are happy.

God wants you to know that He is always watching you, and He is always ready to bless you and protect you.

Dear God, thank You for loving me and keeping Your eye on me!

God watches over
and protects me.

Missy Benfield, Prospect Baptist Church, Albemarle, NC

Love and Hope

The Lord looks after . . . those who put their hope in his love.
—PSALM 33:18

D o you know what hope is? Hope is wanting something to happen (or to be true) and then believing it will!

We can put our hope in Jesus because He will always do what He says. Jesus keeps His promises. We can put our hope in the Bible because everything it says is true. And we can put our hope in God's love, He will always do what is best for us.

We can hope for God to help us and protect us because we know He loves us.

Thank You, God, that because You love me and You never change, I can have hope.

I put my hope in God because He loves me.

Learning to Pray

"When you pray, say: 'Father, we pray that your name will always be kept holy.'"

—LUKE 11:2

J esus' friends wanted to learn how to pray, so they asked the expert—Jesus!

The first lesson Jesus taught them was that they could call God their Father. A father should be someone who loves his children and protects them. Fathers teach their children all kinds of things that are important.

Fathers also teach their children how to pray, just like Jesus taught His friends. Prayer is the way we talk to God, and talking to God every day is important. The best way to learn to pray is to practice!

Thank You, Jesus, for teaching us how to pray.

I will practice praying every day.

Jesus Said, "Go!"

"Go and make followers of all people in the world. Baptize them in the name of the Father and the Son and the Holy Spirit."
—MATTHEW 28:19

You may know that Jesus died and then was raised from the dead. Did you also know that He visited His friends for forty days before He returned to His home in heaven?

Right before Jesus returned to heaven, He gave His friends some very important final instructions. He told them to go and share His love with others so they will believe in Him and follow Him.

Just like His friends back then, Jesus wants us, His friends today, to share His love with people who don't yet know Him. So go and tell your friends how much Jesus loves them!

God, I know You will help me tell others about Jesus. Help them believe and follow Him.

Jesus wants me
to share His
love with others!

Amy Dixon, Liberty Baptist Church, Dublin, GA   219

Knowing God Is Real

You are a God that people cannot see.
—ISAIAH 45:15

We can't see God the way we see ourselves in the mirror, the way we see our friends, or the way we see the trees and the sky. So how do we know He is real?

First, we know God is real because of His amazing creation. Your body didn't just suddenly appear—God made you. The stars in the sky didn't magically appear, and the trees didn't suddenly start to grow—God made them. We cannot see God, but we can see what He created.

We also know God is real because He answers our prayers.

God, I am thankful that I can know You exist because of all You created.

God's creation shows that He is real.

Amy Dixon, Liberty Baptist Church, Dublin, GA

A Reflection of God

God created human beings in his image.... God blessed them and said, "Have many children and grow in number."
—GENESIS 1:27–28

God created people in His image. That means we are like God in some ways, and it means that people can learn about God when they see how we live. Because we are like God, we can choose to do what is right. We can also help people know who God is when we love them—when we are kind, patient, and helpful; when we get along with people; and when we forgive.

God is very happy when others can understand who He is by the way we live.

God, since I am created in Your image, help me be a good reflection of You.

I want to reflect
God with my life.

He Only Speaks Truth!

"I am the Lord, and I speak the truth. I say what is right."
—ISAIAH 45:19

Have you ever told a lie or said something that wasn't true so you wouldn't get in trouble?

Did you know that God can never tell a lie? It's impossible for God to tell a lie, and that means everything He says is always right and always truthful. It also means that God will keep every promise He has made—and He made a lot of promises.

We can trust what God teaches us in the Bible. We can trust that He will take good care of us and always love us because that's what the Bible says.

Dear God, knowing that You always speak the truth helps me trust You.

God wants me to tell the truth!

How Do We Love God?

"One must love God with all his heart, all his mind, and all his strength."

—MARK 12:33

I n the Bible God tells us how to live in a way that is good for us and that makes Him happy.

God's most important command is to love Him with every part of who we are. Loving God with all our hearts means loving Him more than we love anyone or anything else. Loving God with all our minds means we keep learning about God. Loving God with all our strength means serving God with the abilities He has given us.

And the reason we can love God like this is because He loved us first.

Dear God, please teach me to love You with all of my heart, mind, and strength.

I want to love God
with all I have.

Amy Dixon, Liberty Baptist Church, Dublin, GA

Good News

*The followers went everywhere in the world and told the
Good News to people. And the Lord helped them.*
—MARK 16:20

All of us love to hear good news. What is some good news that made you smile?

"We're going to Grandma's house!"

"It's a snow day! No school!"

"Pizza for dinner tonight!"

There are lots of kinds of good news, but have you heard the best news? The best news in the entire world is that Jesus loves us and has forgiven us for all our sins. People we share that best news with will be glad we did.

To which friend today will you say, "Do you know that Jesus loves you?"

*Jesus, thank You for loving me, forgiving me, and
helping me tell my friends about You.*

> The best news
> is that Jesus
> loves me!

Tim Anderson, Clements Baptist Church, Athens, AL

Make Me Willing

Keep me strong by giving me a willing spirit.
—Psalm 51:12

Have you ever had a hard time obeying your parents? All of us have. Sometimes we just don't want to do what Mom or Dad asks!

Jesus is sad when we don't obey our parents. But if you ask Jesus to forgive you when you don't obey, He will.

Also whenever you disobey, tell your parents you're sorry you disobeyed them. Ask them to pray that God will make you want to obey them and Him.

When you are willing to obey, God gives you the strength you need to do what you're asked to do.

Jesus, please make me willing to always obey You and my parents.

I feel happy when I obey!

I Am Holding Your Hand

*"I am the Lord your God. I am holding your right hand.
And I tell you, 'Don't be afraid. I will help you.'"*
—Isaiah 41:13

On the first day of Vacation Bible School, Tim felt nervous. When his big sister took his hand, he felt much braver. Any time Tim was afraid of the dark, his mom held his hand until he wasn't afraid anymore.

Jesus holds our hands so we aren't afraid in the dark or anywhere else. We won't feel Jesus' hand the way we feel Mom's or Dad's, but this is the Bible's way of saying that Jesus is always with us to keep us from being afraid. When you feel afraid, know that Jesus is holding your hand.

Jesus, thank You for always being with me when I feel afraid.

I do not have to be afraid with Jesus.

Follow the Leader

"All people will know that you are my followers if you love each other."

—JOHN 13:35

D o you like to play follow the leader? Which do you like better—being the leader or a follower? There are good things about both, right?

There are a lot of good things about Jesus being the Leader we follow in life. The best way we show people that we are following Jesus is by loving them—by doing things like being kind, sharing, helping them, and praying for them. Jesus will help us love people the way He wants us to.

Jesus really is the best Leader you and your family can follow for life.

Jesus, when I read my Bible, please show me how to follow You the way I should.

I want to follow Jesus!

It's All About God's Love

*Hearing good news from a faraway place is like
having a cool drink when you are tired.*
—PROVERBS 25:25

You probably know some good stories from the Bible. Maybe Daniel in the lions' den or Jesus walking on water is one of your favorites.

From beginning to end, the Bible teaches about God's love for us. We read that God forgives our sins, protects us, provides for us, guides us, heals us, and has a place in heaven waiting for us.

The Bible is all about God's love! It's full of stories that are more wonderful than a cold glass of lemonade after doing chores on a hot day.

*Jesus, thank You for my Bible and the
very good news it contains.*

The Bible tells us
about God's love.

Tim Anderson, Clements Baptist Church, Athens, AL

Right Words

The right word spoken at the right time is as beautiful as gold apples in a silver bowl.
—PROVERBS 25:11

Jesus wants us to love Him and to love the people He puts into our lives. One of the best things we can do to love people is to speak kindly to them. And it doesn't take any more energy to say nice words than it does to say mean words, does it?

As the Bible says, nice words are as beautiful as shiny apples. They make people smile and laugh. Nice words can help and encourage them. We can use nice words in notes we write to people and when we pray for them.

Our nice words make Jesus happy.

Jesus, help me always speak kind words to people so their lives are more beautiful.

I want to speak kind words!

The One True God

"You must not have any other gods except me."
—DEUTERONOMY 5:7

Have you heard of the Ten Commandments? Today's verse is commandment number one—and it's the most important commandment of the ten. Loving God is the best thing we can do in life.

But sometimes we are tempted to worship a false god. That means we make someone or something else more important than the real God. We need to keep God the most important part of our lives, tell Him we love Him, pray to Him, obey Him, and worship Him.

The God we know from reading the Bible is the one true God. He is Lord!

Lord, I love You. Please teach me to make You most important in my life.

I want to love God with all my heart.

Be Ready

*Always be ready to answer everyone who asks
you to explain about the hope you have.*
—1 PETER 3:15

P eople who know Jesus should be different
from people who don't know Jesus. We should
be nicer, more joyful, more patient, and more
loving. When we are like that, people may be
puzzled. They may wonder why we are so patient
and kind. Life is hard for everyone, so when people
see us being joyful, they may want to know what
our secret is.

So when they ask, "Why are you so happy?" we
can say, "Because Jesus loves me!" That can be a
chance to tell those people that Jesus loves them
too.

*Lord, please help me explain the Bible's
message of hope whenever I have a chance.*

I will be ready to
talk about Jesus.

Dr. Ted Traylor, Olive Baptist Church, Pensacola, FL   231

God Will Keep Me Safe

You will feel safe because there is hope. You will look around and rest in safety.

—Job 11:18

Sometimes sad things and hard things happen in our lives. A lot of sad and tough things happened in Job's life, and there is a book in the Bible about what happened to Job.

In that book, Job showed us how to live when life is not easy. Everyone will have hard days, but we can learn from Job to choose to trust God and know that God will keep you safe during those tough days.

No matter what has happened and no matter how sad we are, we can decide to trust God to take care of us and keep us safe.

Lord, in hard times, help me trust You to take care of me.

God will keep me safe.

Dr. Ted Traylor, Olive Baptist Church, Pensacola, FL

The Best Creation of All

God decided to give us life through the word of truth. He wanted us to be the most important of all the things he made.
—JAMES 1:18

G od made light, the sky, the land, and the oceans. He made the stars and the planets, the sun and the moon. He made all the plants and all the animals that live on land—and all the plants and all the animals that live in the water. And He saved the best for last: He made human beings. He made you and me.

God created us so we can love Him. And because God loves us, He teaches us the truth about who He is so we can love Him well.

Lord, thank You for making people the most important of all the amazing things You created.

God created me!

What Should I Say?

Pray that when I speak, God will give me words so that I can tell the secret truth of the Good News without fear.
—Ephesians 6:19

Are you a little shy about sharing the Good News? Even adults are! That's why Paul, the adult who wrote the verse above, asked people to pray for the times he would share the good news.

When you—like Paul—pray about what to say, you can count on God to help you say the right things. God wants you to tell people that He loves them. So when you want to tell someone about Jesus, pray and ask God to help you. God is faithful, and He will always help you.

Lord, please help me share the good news so people understand and want Your love.

God will give me the right words.

We Have Good News

Jesus said to the followers, "Go everywhere in the world. Tell the Good News to everyone."
—MARK 16:15

Who is the good news about? Jesus, God's Son. Why did Jesus come to earth? To die on the cross as punishment for our sins so we could call God *Father.*

What happened after Jesus died and was buried? He came back to life.

What do I have to do to call God *Father*? First, realize that you sin. Second, believe that Jesus died on the cross and came back to life. Third, ask Him to be your King for life.

God loves us, forgives us, and has a place in heaven for us. This is good news!

God, please give me courage to tell this good news to people who need Your love.

I want to tell the good news to others.

Dr. Ted Traylor, Olive Baptist Church, Pensacola, FL

Talking About Jesus

The one who plants and the one who waters have the same purpose. And each will be rewarded for his own work.
—1 CORINTHIANS 3:8

Think about how different you are from your friends and family. Your laugh is different from everyone else's. Your eyes are different. Your belly button is different. Even the tiny lines on your fingertips are different! God made all of His people one-of-a-kind and different from everyone else.

But as different as we are, we all have the same purpose. And that purpose is to tell everybody we know about Jesus. Whether you're the first person to tell someone about Jesus or the second, third, or fourth, God is pleased we are talking about Jesus.

Dear God, help me talk about Jesus.

I will tell my friends about Jesus!

Pastor Joe Donahue, First Baptist Church, Lavaca, AR

God's Plan Is the Best Plan

We know that in everything God works for the good of those who love him. They are the people God called, because that was his plan.
—ROMANS 8:28

Think about all the things you did yesterday. Maybe some things you did were fun, and you laughed a lot. Maybe some things were hard, and God helped you. And maybe other things made you sad, and God was sad too.

When things happen that make us sad, we can be sure that God will bring good out of them. God has a good plan for your life. He wants to make you more like Jesus (that's pretty amazing!), and He wants you to know joy because you know Jesus.

Dear God, thank You for making me a little more like Jesus every day!

God has good plans for my life.

Story Time with Jesus

Jesus used stories to tell all these things to the people. He always used stories to teach people.
—MATTHEW 13:34

What is your favorite Bible story about Jesus? Do you know that you can learn something from every story about Him?

Jesus wants to teach you something in every story you read. He can teach you that He is powerful, wise, loving, patient, kind, joyful, and good. He can teach you that He wants you to pray, read the Bible, obey His commands (and Mom and Dad), love God, and love people. Every time you read the Bible, figure out what lesson you can learn, and you will become a very wise follower of Jesus!

Dear Jesus, help me learn more about You as I read the Bible every day.

I can learn from Jesus!

The Most Important Truth

There are many other things that Jesus did. If every one of them were written down, I think the whole world would not be big enough for all the books that would be written.
—JOHN 21:25

Jesus' friend John wrote about Jesus' life, but John told us that he didn't write about all the wonderful things Jesus did.

John told us about some very amazing things Jesus did. We learn, for instance, that Jesus healed people, fed five thousand people with five loaves of bread and two fish, walked on water, raised Lazarus from the dead, and taught people how to be His followers.

We don't know everything Jesus did, but what we do know makes us sure He is God's Son. And that is the most important thing we can ever know!

Dear Jesus, thank You that I know the most important truth ever: You are God's Son!

Jesus is God's Son.

Pastor Joe Donahue, First Baptist Church, Lavaca, AR

239

Worshipping God

Children, come and listen to me. I will teach you to worship the Lord.

—PSALM 34:11

Did you know that there are different ways to worship God? One way we can worship God is through music. God loves to hear us sing our praises to Him. What is your favorite song to sing or listen to when you want to worship God?

King David sang and wrote worship songs to God. The book of Psalms is full of David's worship songs. Another way to worship God is to praise Him. When you sing worship songs, you are praising God and telling Him that you love Him. The Bible lists other ways we can worship God. Ask your parents to tell you about more ways to worship God.

God, thank You for teaching me how to worship You.

I can sing and worship God wherever I go!

Pastor Joe Donahue, First Baptist Church, Lavaca, AR

He Listens to Me

The Lord sees the good people. He listens to their prayers.
—PSALM 34:15

Jesus listens to you because you are very special to Him. He is never in a hurry when you speak to Him. He is interested in every single word you say to Him and every story you tell Him. He listens to you when you are sad or lonely. And He listens to you when you are excited and happy.

When we listen to others, we show that we think they are important. Today you can show others they are special by listening more closely to what they say to you!

Jesus, thank You for always listening to me. Help me to listen closely to others.

Jesus always hears me!

You Are Never Alone

The Lord is close to the brokenhearted. He saves those whose spirits have been crushed.
—PSALM 34:18

It's easy to feel all alone when we are sad, isn't it? And a lot of things can make us sad: someone's mean words, canceled plans, losing your favorite toy, or crashing on your new bike.

The great news in today's verse is that you are never alone. Whether you are sad or happy, or if something bad happens in your family or at school, God is near you!

You can't see the air you breathe, and you can't see God. But even when you feel sad and lonely, you will know that God is with you.

✧✧ *Lord, thank You for loving me and for comforting me when I am sad.* ✧

I can tell God
how I'm feeling.

Something That Lasts Forever

The grass dies, and the flowers fall. But the word of our God will live forever.

—ISAIAH 40:8

Things around us do not last very long. In the fall of every year, leaves on the trees change color. The leaves eventually turn brown and fall off. Sometimes grass will turn brown in the winter. Beautiful flowers—in the garden or in a vase—droop and wilt and die.

But there is one thing that will last through every season, every year, every century—and that is God's Word. In fact, the Bible will last forever! Be sure to read the Bible each day because something that lasts forever is a very important something.

Dear God, thank You for the Bible and its truth that will last forever!

Read the Bible to know God better.

Dr. Brian and Bonnie Stowe,
First Baptist Church Plant City, Plant City, FL

It's the Truth

What we told you were not just smart stories that someone invented. But we saw the greatness of Jesus with our own eyes.
—2 PETER 1:16

D o you like stories? Maybe you like to make up your own stories. Maybe you like to have someone read you stories. We like stories where the good guy wins or where everyone is happy at the end. But these stories may not always be true.

Did you know that every single story in the Bible is true? Your favorite stories about Noah, Moses, Joshua, Ruth, David, Esther, Jonah, Jesus, Peter, and Paul are all absolutely true! And the stories we read in The New Testament show us how great our Jesus is!

Thank You, Lord, that every word and every story in the Bible is true.

The Bible is true.

Dr. Brian and Bonnie Stowe,
First Baptist Church Plant City, Plant City, FL

The Flashlight for My Life

Your word is like a lamp for my feet and a light for my way.
—PSALM 119:105

Have you ever walked through your house when it is dark? It isn't easy, and it can be scary. You know you might trip over a toy, step on a LEGO piece, or walk into a wall. But if you have a flashlight, you do not feel scared. That flashlight helps you see the good steps to take.

Today's verse tells us that the Bible—also called God's Word—is like a flashlight. The Bible helps us know what the smart choices and good steps are in life. God's Word helps us feel safe and be wise!

Dear God, thank You for using the Bible to help me make good choices.

The Bible is a light for my life.

My Favorite Meal

"A person does not live only by eating bread. But a person lives by everything the Lord says."
—MATTHEW 4:4

What is your favorite meal? God has given us all kinds of great food to eat. We like food because it tastes good, but food does the important job of giving our body fuel so we can play, help with chores, and do schoolwork. Eating healthy food three times a day will make our bodies strong.

The Bible will make our love for Jesus strong. When we read the Bible, we learn how to have good thoughts and make good decisions. Reading the Bible and eating very healthy food will always be good for you!

God, help me enjoy reading the Bible as much as I love eating my favorite meal.

God's Word is important to me!

Tell Somebody!

Shout out loud the good news. Shout it out and don't be afraid.
—ISAIAH 40:9

What is something good that recently happened to you? Did you tell others? It is fun to share good news, isn't it?

The Bible is good news. The Bible is the best news because it tells us that God loves you and all people. That's amazing and great and wonderful news. God loves you and He always will. There is nothing you can do to make Him stop loving you. Nothing!

Now think about the people you know. Who needs to hear the good news that God loves them? Tell those people!

Dear God, thank You for the very good news that You love me.

I want to tell the great news!

Dr. Brian and Bonnie Stowe,
First Baptist Church Plant City, Plant City, FL

247

Jesus the Teacher

Jesus saw the crowds who were there. He went up on a hill and sat down. His followers came to him. Jesus taught the people.
—MATTHEW 5:1–2

I magine having Jesus as your Sunday school teacher! That would be crazy and very cool!

Whenever Jesus taught, many people listened. They were very interested in what He had to say because He spoke about God. Jesus taught about love, forgiveness, and helping our neighbors. Jesus taught about praying and trusting Him. He taught that God needs to be more important than anything or anyone else. And Jesus taught about living a life that would make God happy.

In the Bible we can read what Jesus taught, and we can learn from His teachings too!

Jesus, thank You that You use the Bible to teach me. ✦

I want to learn about Jesus!

Mrs. Amy Boyles,
First Baptist Church Snellville, Snellville, GA

God's Comfort

"Those who are sad now are happy. God will comfort them."
—MATTHEW 5:4

Who do you talk to when you are sad? You probably talk to your mom or dad. Maybe you talk to a special friend.

Did you know you can also talk to God when you are sad? He can help you feel better when you are sad. (You can also talk to God when you are happy, and He can help you feel even happier!)

God made you, and He loves you. He can feel sad when you are sad (that's called *compassion*), and He can help you feel less sad (that's called *comfort*).

Dear Jesus, thank You for helping me feel better when I am sad.

Jesus cares about how I feel.

Choosing Mercy

"Those who give mercy to others are happy.
Mercy will be given to them."

—MATTHEW 5:7

Your brother wants to play with the toy you are playing with. He's angry and says mean things. Then he grabs it and tries to take it away. That's when Mom says, "Hey, you two! Try to get along!"

Your brother lets go. Will you let him play with the toy? Giving him a turn is mercy: he did not behave nicely, and he does not deserve to have a turn. But when you act with mercy—when you share the toy anyway—you will feel happy inside. And you will be doing what Jesus did.

Thank You, Jesus, for Your kindness and mercy. Help me be kind and give mercy.

> Jesus wants me to
> show mercy.

The Perfect Gift

"Those people who know they have great spiritual needs are happy. The kingdom of heaven belongs to them."
—MATTHEW 5:3

If a girl walking through the woods doesn't know she is lost, it's hard to help her. If the boy doesn't know he's holding the baseball bat wrong, it's hard to help him. If people don't know they need help, it's hard to help them!

Many people don't know they need God's love. They don't know God created in them the need to know His love. Sometimes a hard time in life helps people realize they need to know God. And sometimes God uses people like you and me to help them see they need His love. When we tell them about Jesus, we give them the perfect gift.

Dear God, thank You for helping me know that I need You and Your love!

The perfect gift is Jesus!

Mrs. Amy Boyles,
First Baptist Church Snellville, Snellville, GA

Good Choices

*"Those who want to do right more than anything
else are happy. God will fully satisfy them."*
—MATTHEW 5:6

When you make a good choice, do you feel happy inside? God wants us to feel good when we make good choices.

So whenever you make a good choice—to be kind, to help someone, or to take a minute to pray—God is very happy because He knows good choices are not always easy.

Did you know, though, that God always gives us a way out of every situation where we could make a wrong choice?

Reading your Bible every day will help you know what God says is right—and He will help you do it!

Dear Lord, help me want to do what is right—and then do it.

I want to do
what is right!

Mrs. Amy Boyles,
First Baptist Church Snellville, Snellville, GA

God Is Big!

"Those who are humble are happy. The earth will belong to them."
—MATTHEW 5:5

Can you remember a time when you lay on your back in the grass and looked up at the big sky? It can make you feel pretty small.

Being humble means knowing we *are* pretty small in this big world. It means knowing that anything good we do is because God helps us. And it means helping people who won't ever be able to help us.

Jesus was humble when He left heaven, came to earth, and died on the cross for our sins. We can thank Jesus by loving Him and living in a way that pleases Him.

Thank You, Jesus, for being humble, leaving Your throne in heaven, and dying on the cross.

Jesus wants me
to be humble.

Work for Peace

"Those who work to bring peace are happy. God will call them his sons."

—MATTHEW 5:9

What do you do when someone says something mean or does something to hurt you? What do you do when someone takes something from you? Do you try to get even? Do you try to hurt him back? You may think that will make you happy, but it never will.

Jesus said happiness comes when we love people even when they are mean to us. When we do that, we will look like we are God's children. We belong to Him—and whenever we choose to love people, we will look like we belong to Him!

Dear Jesus, help me live at peace with everyone, even people who are mean.

Jesus wants me to love everyone.

Honoring God

Honor God with your bodies.
—1 CORINTHIANS 6:20

You probably know that God made you. He gave you your eye color and hair color, certain talents (swimming, doing math, drawing), and certain favorites (reading, chocolate, kittens).

Since God made our bodies, it makes sense that He wants us to honor Him with our bodies—but what does that mean? *Honor* means to know that something is good or someone is important and to show respect for that thing or person. We honor our bodies when we take good care of them—when we eat healthy food, exercise, and get enough sleep.

Dear God, the human body You made is amazing. Help me take care of mine!

I will take care of my body because God made it.

Rocky Purvis, Northside Baptist Church, Lexington, SC   255

Growing

Your children will grow like a tree in the grass.
—ISAIAH 44:4

Have you ever planted a seed, made sure it had water, sunlight, and space, and then waited for it to grow? It's incredible that a little seed can grow into something so different and so big. Some seeds become trees so tall you could climb up into their branches.

God made seeds to grow, and God made your body to grow. He also wants you to grow in how well you know Him and how much you love Him. You can help this happen by reading the Bible, praying, memorizing verses, and worshipping God.

Dear Jesus, help me grow to love You more and more each day.

I want to grow and know Jesus better.

Rocky Purvis, Northside Baptist Church, Lexington, SC

Living for Jesus

Everything you say and everything you do should all be done for Jesus your Lord.

—COLOSSIANS 3:17

How do you look at your life? Maybe you think about its different parts: Your life at school. Your life playing sports. Your life with your family. Your life with your friends. Your life at church. Your life with Jesus. A lot of people think like this.

Do you know why we shouldn't think like this? It keeps Jesus outside and away from everything else we're doing—and the Bible says Jesus should be the *reason* for all we do. With everything we say and everything we do, we should be trying to make Him happy. That's putting Jesus first.

Jesus, I want You first in my life so I make You happy with whatever I am doing.

I want to
please Jesus!

Like Father, like Son

"All people will respect the Son the same way they respect the Father."

—JOHN 5:23

L ike father, like son" means that the way a son acts, thinks, or talks is a lot like the way his dad acts, thinks, and talks.

"Like Father, like Son" is definitely true of God and His Son, Jesus. The Son is known for His love, power, kindness, healing, and wisdom. God, Jesus' Father, is also loving, powerful, kind, healing, and wise. When we know Jesus, the Son, we know more about the God, the Father.

And we are to respect Jesus—we are to see how good and important He is—the same way we respect God.

Thank You, God, that I can know You better because I know Jesus.

I want to act, think, and talk more like Jesus!

We Have a Helper

"The Helper will teach you everything. He will
cause you to remember all the things I told you."
—JOHN 14:26

H ave you ever had a helper? That person may
have helped you learn to read, ride a bike, or
throw a fast ball. Maybe that person helped you
clean your room or finish your homework.

You have another Helper who helps you with
other things. That Helper is the Holy Spirit. (After
Jesus went to heaven, He sent us the Holy Spirit.)
One way the Holy Spirit helps everyone who loves
Jesus is by teaching us everything we need to
know about Him. The Holy Spirit also guides us
when we make decisions.

Thank You, Holy Spirit, for teaching me, guiding
me, praying for me, and helping me.

I am glad the Holy
Spirit is my Helper!

God's Beautiful World

When you look up at the sky, you see the sun,
moon and stars.... The Lord your God has made
these things for all people everywhere.
—DEUTERONOMY 4:19

P retend you walk into the kitchen and see a plate of homemade chocolate chip cookies! I bet when you see those cookies, you immediately think of your mom: you know she made them for you. You know she loves you.

After eating a cookie, you walk outside and see the sky, birds, and flowers. When you see God's creation, He wants you to think of Him right away just like you thought of Mom when you saw the cookies. When you notice something beautiful, God wants you to think of Him and His love.

Thank You for creating this wonderful world and
filling it with amazing things You made.

God made
the world!

Amy Cooper, New Vision Baptist Church, Murfreesboro, TN

A Wonderful Gift

Thanks be to God for his gift that is too wonderful to explain.
—2 CORINTHIANS 9:15

Have you ever been given such an incredible gift that you could not think of anything to say after opening it? Maybe you cried or shouted or jumped up and down with excitement.

God has given us *the* best gift ever, and this gift is truly so wonderful that we could never describe it. That gift is Jesus! Because God gave us Jesus to be punished for our sins, we can live in heaven with God forever.

The best gift you will ever get—better than a bicycle, a puppy, or a game system—is Jesus!

Dear God, thank You so very much for the wonderful gift of Your Son.

God's gift to us is Jesus!

Connecting with God

Continue praying. . . . And when you pray, always thank God.
—COLOSSIANS 4:2

Praying is a way for us to stay connected to God—and it's something we can do anytime, day or night. Prayer keeps us thinking about God, doing what God wants us to do, going where He wants us to go, and talking and acting more like Jesus.

Think about walking across a busy street. There is a lot going on all around you. Holding your mom's hand, your dad's hand, or both their hands will keep you safe.

This world can be like a busy street. Praying is like holding God's hand. He will keep you safe.

Dear God, thank You that I can always pray and feel closer to You!

I can pray anytime.

Trust in the Lord

"The person who trusts in the Lord will be blessed. The Lord will show him that he can be trusted."
—JEREMIAH 17:7

D o you know what *trust* means? It means believing that something is good or that people will be honest and do what they say they will do.

So if you trust a chair to hold you up—if you believe it is a good, strong chair—what will you do? You will sit on it.

And if you trust God, you will believe His promises and obey His teachings. The Bible says we will be blessed (or happy) when we trust God—and that God will give us even more reasons to trust Him!

Dear God, I want to trust You more and more each day. Please help me.

I can always trust God!

Amy Cooper, New Vision Baptist Church, Murfreesboro, TN   263

God's Big Hug

If we confess our sins, [God] will forgive our sins.
—1 JOHN 1:9

God is our loving Father who wants and waits to forgive us for the wrong things we do. (The word for those wrong things is *sin*.) But to be forgiven, we have to realize we've done something wrong. After we realize we've done wrong, then we pray to God. We tell God the wrong things we have done, say that we're sorry, and decide not to do those things anymore. This is called *confessing.*

Then, since God is your loving Father, He will forgive you. When He does, you feel so loved. It's like God gives you a big hug!

God, thank You for forgiving my sin and loving me no matter what!

God forgives me when I ask.

Amy Cooper, New Vision Baptist Church, Murfreesboro, TN

Just like a Magnet

Come near to God, and God will come near to you.
—JAMES 4:8

Have you ever seen what happens when you move a magnet near a piece of metal? The metal attaches to the magnet, and it can be hard to get the metal and the magnet apart.

Now imagine that God and you are like a magnet and a piece of metal. He created you to be close to Him, and the closer you get to Him, the closer He comes to you. And once you are close to God, you won't want to go back to being far away. You will only want to get closer!

Dear God, thank You for creating me—and wanting me—to be close to You!

I want to get closer to God.

God Sings About You

The Lord will be happy with you. You will rest in his love. He will sing and be joyful about you.
—ZEPHANIAH 3:17

Does it make you happy to be with people you love? Do you smile a lot? Do you want to do a cartwheel or celebrate with fireworks?

Did you know that God is very happy to be with you? He created you, He loves you, and He enjoys your company. He loves it when you read the Bible and pray to Him. God doesn't do cartwheels or set off fireworks to celebrate you, but He doesn't hide the joy He has in you. God—the Creator of the universe—sings and is joyful about you!

Dear Lord, thank You for singing about me because You love me so much.

I make God happy!

God's Name Is Special

"So when you pray, you should pray like this: 'Our Father in heaven, we pray that your name will always be kept holy.'"
—MATTHEW 6:9

There is no one in the whole world who is just like you. Your name is part of what makes you who you are! What if someone used your name in a mean way? What if someone made fun of your name or used it as a bad word? That would be sad.

God's name is very special too. Making fun of God's name or using it as a bad word would be even sadder than someone using yours in a mean way. God's name deserves respect and honor. That is why Jesus taught His followers to pray that God's name will always be used in a kind, loving way. We need to keep God's name special because it is His!

Dear Lord, I praise You! Your name is the most important name of all.

God's name is special.

Sue Barksdale, The Church on Rush Creek, Arlington, TX

God's Promise

"I promise that my Spirit and my words that I give you will never leave you."

—ISAIAH 59:21

P romises are good only when the person making the promise keeps the promise.

In today's verse, God made an important promise, and because God is perfect, we know He always keeps His promises. God promised that His Holy Spirit and words of truth will never leave His people. That means His children will never be alone and they will always have His help when they need it.

Rainbows remind us that God's promises are true. Next time you see a brightly colored rainbow, remember God loves you very much and you are never alone!

Dear Lord, thank You that Your Spirit and words of truth will be with me always.

God promises to never leave me!

Sue Barksdale, The Church on Rush Creek, Arlington, TX

Obey Your Parents

Listen to your father, who gave you life. And do not forget your mother when she is old.
—Proverbs 23:22

Think about this: of all the parents in the world, God gave you your mom and your dad. God chose your parents just for you to love you and take care of you.

That's one reason why God wants you to listen to your parents and obey them. Sometimes obeying is hard because you want to do things your way. But the Bible says the right way to live is always to obey. God is pleased when you love your parents and do what they ask you to do.

Dear Lord, thank You for my parents. Help me obey them.

I want to obey my mom and dad.

Peek-a-Boo

God's word judges the thoughts and feelings in our hearts. Nothing in all the world can be hidden from God.
—HEBREWS 4:12–13

Have you played peek-a-boo with a baby? You hid your face behind a blanket, moved it away quickly, called "peek-a-boo!" and she giggled and laughed! You were never gone, but she thought you were.

You may have tried to play peek-a-boo with God. You might have thought that you could hide the wrong thing you did, but you couldn't. You'll never be able to hide your sin from God. He won't let you because He wants you to talk to Him about the wrong thing so He can forgive you.

Dear Lord, when I do something wrong, help me pray to You instead of trying to hide from You.

I can't hide my sin from God.

God's Super Power

Oh, Lord God, you made the skies and the earth.
You made them with your very great power.
—JEREMIAH 32:17

D o you like to pretend you are a superhero? Maybe you pretend to fly, lift mountains, climb buildings, or save cities.

It's fun to hear stories about superheroes, but they are not real people. God is the only One with real super powers—and His power is amazing. For instance, God made the world with just His words. God didn't have to put on any special suit or use any special tool. He just called for the earth and the skies to start being—and there they were!

We serve a mighty God!

Lord, You made the heavens and earth using only Your words. Your power is the greatest ever!

God is better than
any superhero.

Jesus Doesn't Change

Jesus Christ is the same yesterday, today, and forever.
—HEBREWS 13:8

D o you have a toy that doesn't look like it did when it was new? It probably has scratches or might even be broken. Your toy isn't the same as it used to be.

Maybe you have a favorite stuffed animal that you love a lot, but it isn't quite as fluffy as it once was.

The Bible says the Lord Jesus will always be the same as He used to be. That means Jesus will always love you, always be strong, and always be with you. Things change, but the Lord Jesus never changes.

Dear Lord Jesus, thank You for never changing and for always loving me.

Jesus never changes!

Dr. Bryan Smith, First Baptist Church, Roanoke, VA

God Did It

In the beginning God created the sky and the earth.
—GENESIS 1:1

When you look out your window, what do you see? The sky? Trees? Grass? Flowers? Maybe mountains or the beach? Maybe the neighbor's dog or birds or bunnies or squirrels?

Did you know that God made *all* of it? He made everything . . . out of nothing! Only God can create something new from nothing at all. He made the whole earth—and He made you too. He is your Creator and the Creator of this big world and everything on it. Thank God for making the sky, the earth, and you!

Dear God, thank You for making everything. Thank You for making me.

God made everything.

Jesus Can Use You

Here is a boy with five loaves of barley bread and two little fish. But that is not enough for so many people.
—JOHN 6:9

Five thousand people had spent the day with Jesus, and now they were hungry. But they didn't have anything to eat.

That's when a boy's lunch was used. Instead of eating his five loaves of bread and two little fish, the boy's lunch was offered. Jesus thanked God for the bread and fish, and then Jesus used it to feed thousands of people—enough people to fill half of a football field! There was even food left over!

Jesus can use you to help people. Ask Him how.

Dear Lord, please use me to help others.

Jesus can use me to share His love.

Thank You, Lord

[The Lord] has done great and wonderful things for you. You have seen them with your own eyes.
—DEUTERONOMY 10:21

Did you know that God does "great and wonderful things" for us every single day?

God gives us the food we eat, the clothes we wear, and a family who loves us. He created a beautiful world for us to explore and amazing bodies that can see and hear, run and jump.

We could name a lot of other good things, but the greatest thing God has done was send His Son, Jesus Christ, to die for us. Jesus took the punishment for our sins. Now we are forgiven, and we can talk to God as our Father.

Dear Lord, thank You for all of the wonderful things you have done.

I can see God's wonderful world all around me.

Dr. Bryan Smith, First Baptist Church, Roanoke, VA

God's Rainbow Promise

*"I am putting my rainbow in the clouds. It is the
sign of the agreement between me and the earth."*
—GENESIS 9:13

D o you like seeing rainbows in the sky?
Rainbows usually appear after the rain stops.
Rainbows are always beautiful, but did you know
that they are in the sky to remind us of a promise?

The Bible teaches that God gave us rainbows to
remind us that He would never again let there be a
flood that would destroy the earth and everything
living on it, like there was when Noah built the ark.

A rainbow is a reminder of God's promise, and
God always keeps His promises. That's why we can
always believe everything God promises us in the
Bible.

*Thank You, God, for always
keeping Your promises.*

Rainbows remind
me that God
keeps His promises.

Dr. Bryan Smith, First Baptist Church, Roanoke, VA

Getting Ready

This is the voice of a man who calls out: "Prepare in the desert the way for the Lord."

—ISAIAH 40:3

When company comes, we clean up the house and fix dinner. We prepare for our friends' visit. When we go outside to play, we put on sunscreen and tennis shoes. We prepare for some fun!

From where he lived in the desert, John the Baptist prepared people to hear what Jesus would teach. John told people to stop sinning, and they learned that they needed to be forgiven for their sins. They wanted to get ready for Jesus. Then they were prepared to accept Jesus as the One who would save them from punishment for their sins.

Dear Jesus, please prepare me! I want to always be ready to learn from You.

Help me be
ready for You.

God Is with Us

Surely the Lord is in this place. But I did not know it. . . . It is surely the house of God and the gate of heaven.
—GENESIS 28:16–17

Today's key verse comes from a story about Jacob. Jacob was all alone one night, and He had a special dream about angels. When he woke up, he couldn't see God, but he knew God was with him.

You can't see God either, but that doesn't mean He isn't with you. In fact, He's really with us all the time. God is always watching over you. He loves you and has promised to never leave you alone. No matter where you are, God is with you in every place and at any time.

Dear God, I can't see You, but I know You are watching over me. Thank You!

I am glad that God is always watching over me!

We Need One Another

If the whole body were an eye, the body would not be able to hear. If the whole body were an ear, the body would not be able to smell anything.
—1 CORINTHIANS 12:17

Touch your nose. Now imagine your nose is another mouth. What if your ears had a tongue and some teeth? That would be crazy! God gave us eyes and ears so we could see and hear. Every part of our bodies has a purpose, and those parts work together.

God calls the people who love Him "the body of Christ." Every one of us has a purpose, and we work together to share God's love and truth in the world. Some people teach Sunday school, some feed hungry people, and others pray for the sick and hurting. You have a special purpose too!

Dear God, thank You for giving me this purpose: to share Your love and truth.

We need to work together.

Dallas White,
First Baptist Church Woodstock, Woodstock, GA

Giving Generously

The good person gives without holding back.
—PROVERBS 21:26

Family, friends, a place to live, food to eat—the Bible teaches that every good gift comes from God. And when God gives gifts, He doesn't hold anything back. He even gave us His Son to take our punishment for our sin so that we would have the gifts of being forgiven and knowing we'll go to heaven.

When God gives us things, He is happy when we share those gifts. And He's even happier when we don't share just a little, but when we share generously, which means sharing without holding back.

Dear God, You've given me a lot of good gifts. Help me to share them generously.

I want to share all the gifts God gives me!

Dallas White,
First Baptist Church Woodstock, Woodstock, GA

God Does Great Things!

The Lord does great things. Those people who love them think about them.

—PSALM 111:2

Did you have a good time at your last birthday party? Did your family take a great vacation during the summer? Maybe God gave you the teacher you wanted.

You have a heavenly Father who loves you and loves to do great things for you. Remembering all the great things God has done for you in the past will help you trust Him.

God will always be powerful and good and loving. You can count on God to do great things today and tomorrow and forever!

Dear God, thank You for doing the great things You have done and will do.

God does great things!

Safe Places

You are my hiding place. You protect me from my troubles.
—Psalm 32:7

King David needed hiding places. When he was a shepherd, he knew the dangers of wild animals. Before becoming king, he knew the dangers of enemy soldiers. David also knew the danger of not confessing his sin: it would make him feel sick!

You probably don't have wild animals or enemy soldiers after you, but maybe there's a bully at school, or homework feels like an enemy, or you have sin to confess. Know that God is your "hiding place," your safe place to go.

Dear God, thank You for protecting me from my troubles.

God is my safe place.

Playing Forever

"The streets will be filled with boys and girls playing."
—ZECHARIAH 8:5

Have you ever thought about what heaven would be like? You may not know this, but when the Bible talks about heaven, it says that "the streets will be filled with boys and girls playing." Doesn't that sound like a great place?

God talked about kids playing as a way of telling us that heaven will be a place of joy and laughter. Does that make you want to spend forever there? It should! That sounds like a very happy place!

If we love Jesus, we will get to spend forever with God in heaven. In that special place we call heaven, you will be able to run and play forever.

Dear Jesus, thank You for this picture of heaven, where I'll be with You forever.

Heaven is
a place of joy.

Dallas White,
First Baptist Church Woodstock, Woodstock, GA

Can You See in the Dark?

I saw that being wise is certainly better than being foolish, just as light is better than darkness.
—ECCLESIASTES 2:13

You walk into a dark room. You think you can find your way, so you don't turn on the light. You take a step, you take another step, and that's when your toe hits something hard, and it hurts! Ouch! It would have been better to turn on the light first, so you could have seen which steps to take.

Just like a light can help you walk through a dark room, the Bible can help you walk the way God wants you to walk and live the way He wants you to live. It is better to live your life with God, just like it is better to turn on the light in the darkness.

Dear God, please help me understand the Bible so I can be wise.

The Bible is a light and a guide for my life.

Pam Agee,
First Baptist Church Woodstock, Woodstock, GA

God Makes Us Strong

*The people who trust the Lord will become strong
again.... They will run without needing rest.*
—ISAIAH 40:31

Have you ever worried that you were not strong enough to help or to do what someone asked you to do? Have you ever wondered if you were strong enough to help God if He asked? You can trust that God will give you the strength to do whatever He has asked you to do.

When you trust God and obey Him, God will give you strength. He will make not only your body strong enough to help but He will also give you a strong heart and mind. God will give you the strength to keep on going, to keep serving Him, and to keep loving others.

*Dear Lord, thank You for making
me strong when I trust in You.*

**I will trust the
Lord and be strong.**

Broken Things Become New

"Look at the new thing I am going to do."
—ISAIAH 43:19

Daaaaad!" cried Emma. "Jack stepped on my LEGO house and broke it all to pieces!"

"I'm sorry that happened, Emma," said Dad, "but you know what? We are going to build something new together, and it will be even better than before."

That is what our heavenly Father does for us. First, we ask God to forgive our sins. Then, we tell Jesus we want to follow Him all our lives. He makes us better than before: He makes us brand new and more able to love Him and more able to love people!

Dear heavenly Father, thank You for making me more able to love.

My heavenly Father makes me a new person inside.

Happy Inside—Smile Outside

Happiness makes a person smile. But sadness breaks a person's spirit.

—PROVERBS 15:13

How do you tell if people are thinking of something that makes them happy? The big smiles you see on their faces, right? When we feel happy on the inside, our faces show it on the outside: we smile!

When you feel sad, you probably have a harder time smiling. (We all do!) But there is a cure for that. Here's something that can always make you smile: God loves you! And His love is like a big hug on the inside that is always there to make you happy.

Dear God, thank You for loving me. Your love is always a reason to smile.

God's love makes me happy!

Pam Agee,
First Baptist Church Woodstock, Woodstock, GA

God Hears and Answers Prayers

When a good man prays, great things happen.
—JAMES 5:16

S ometimes it's hard to tell how strong something is. You don't know how tight the lid of the pickle jar is until you try to open it. You don't know how strong the tree's roots are until the winds blow hard.

And you don't always know how strong your prayers are, but you have God's promise that when you pray, great things happen. Sometimes you will see those great things right away; other times you'll have to wait. But all the time you can trust that God is answering in the best possible way and at the perfect time.

Dear God, thank You that You make great things happen when I pray to You.

God listens when I pray.

Pam Agee,
First Baptist Church Woodstock, Woodstock, GA

Joy

Be full of joy in the Lord always.
—PHILIPPIANS 4:4

We all have chores to do, and Saturday morning may be time for chores in your family.

Of course you may not *feel* happy when Mom says it's time to clean your room. But you have reasons to *be* happy: you have a bed to sleep in, toys to play with, clothes to wear, a family who loves you, and a God who loves you.

That is *joy*. We can know joy even when we feel lonely or sad or are cleaning our room. That's because we can always choose to be joyful about the fact that God loves us.

Dear Lord, You and Your love are good reasons for me to be full of joy.

I will choose to be joyful!

A Happy Heart

A happy heart is like good medicine.
—PROVERBS 17:22

Medicine can help us feel better when we are sick. God tells us there is something else that can also make us feel better, and that is a happy heart. A heart that thinks happy thoughts is like good medicine.

What can you do to have a happy heart? Look at God's blessings all around you. Be happy when other people are happy. Be kind, share, and help people. And all that is a lot better than pouting, whining, and complaining!

Living with a happy heart is good for you—and for your family.

Jesus, I want to have happy thoughts. Help me notice the good things all around me.

I will have a happy heart.

Words That Taste like Candy

*Pleasant words are like a honeycomb. They make
a person happy and healthy.*

—PROVERBS 16:24

What's your favorite candy bar? It sure tastes sweet and yummy, doesn't it? Does eating that candy bar make you happy? Did you know that sweet words can make you even happier?

Think about when Dad says "I love you," or when Mom says "Thanks for setting the table," or when a friend says "I'm glad we're friends." Words that are sweet make a person feel happy. Mean words make a person feel unhappy.

God wants us to speak to people with words that will make them smile just like their favorite candy bar does!

God, please help me say nice things so my words are sweet and yummy.

Kind words make
people happy.

Keith and Nichole Boggs,
Real Momentum Ministries, Inc., Canton, GA

Lord, Show Me Your Muscles

"I will make you strong and will help you."
—ISAIAH 41:10

Has your mommy ever lifted you up to sit in a shopping cart? Has your daddy ever picked you up and put you on his shoulders so you could see over a crowd of people?

Mom and Dad are strong, but God is stronger. In fact, nothing is too hard for God. He can do anything He wants to do—anything that is good for the people He loves.

God promises to make you strong, but He is not talking about strong arms. God will help you grow strong in your love for Him and in your faith in Him.

God, thank You for promising to help me have a strong faith in You.

I will follow God.

Keith and Nichole Boggs,
Real Momentum Ministries, Inc., Canton, GA

All People

All people have sinned and are not good enough for God's glory.

—ROMANS 3:23

Today's key verse says, *"All* people have sinned"! Are you surprised to know everyone has sinned? Sin is not just lying, cheating, or stealing. Sin is also having bad thoughts and not sharing and saying mean things. Sin is hitting, kicking, and pushing when you are angry. And disobeying your parents is sin.

God has never sinned, but we sin all the time. Even the nicest person you know sins sometimes and needs God's forgiveness. And that's why Jesus died on the cross. He took our punishment. Now God can forgive our sins.

God, I know You don't like my sin—and I don't either. Please help me not sin.

I can be forgiven only because of Jesus.

Becoming a Child of God

Some people did accept [Jesus]. They believed in him. To them he gave the right to become children of God.
　　　　　　　　　　　　　　　　　　　　—JOHN 1:12

We all like to belong. We like to belong to a team or a club or a family.

Jesus taught that if you believe He is God's Son, you can belong to God. Jesus wants you to believe in Him. He loves you and wants you to become a child of God.

And what a blessing to be a child of God! He will help you be more like Jesus. And He will help you obey Him and your parents. He will always love you and take care of you because He is a good Father.

God, thank You for showing me Jesus is Your Son so I can be Your child.

I am a child of God!

Obedience Is . . .

Children, obey your parents the way the Lord
wants. This is the right thing to do.
—EPHESIANS 6:1

O bedience is doing what you are told to do, doing it when you are told to do it, and doing it with a happy heart. Your obedience makes Mom and Dad happy, and your obedience makes God happy.

In fact, did you know that God promises that life will go well for children who obey their parents? Clearly, obeying your parents is important to God. He will bless you when you obey Mom and Dad.

One more thing: Mom, Dad, and the Lord have good reasons for their rules and instructions. So do the right thing and obey!

Dear God, help me to obey my parents immediately and cheerfully even when I don't want to.

I want to obey my
parents quickly
and cheerfully.

Keith and Nichole Boggs,
Real Momentum Ministries, Inc., Canton, GA

295

Saying and Doing

Our love should not be only words and talk. Our love must be true love. And we should show that love by what we do.
—1 JOHN 3:18

Moms and dads *say* "I love you" to their kids. And moms and dads *show* their love by what they do.

Parents show their love by taking care of their children. They go to work to earn money. They make meals, help with homework, buy clothes (and wash them), take you places, and pray with you.

Moms and dads both say and show their love, and God does too: He *said* in the Bible He loves you, and He *showed* this love for you when He sent His Son, Jesus, to die on the cross as punishment for your sins.

Dear Jesus, help me tell people I love them and show them with my actions.

I want to speak and show love!

Pastor Greg Pulling, Journey Christian Fellowship, New Kent, VA

Making Friends

A person who loves innocent thoughts and kind words will have even the king as a friend.
—PROVERBS 22:11

Do you know anyone who always speaks kind words and thinks about how to be nice to other people?

If you do, that person probably has lots of friends. Everyone likes people who are nice and who are not thinking only of themselves.

Jesus is the best friend ever because He is always kind and never self-centered. He was kind when He healed, fed, and taught people. He was thinking more about others than Himself when He died on the cross.

God can help us be a good friend like Jesus is.

Dear Jesus, help me to always be kind and think about others.

I want to be a good friend.

Right and Wrong

All Scripture is inspired by God and is useful for teaching . . . how to live right.

—2 TIMOTHY 3:16

In the Bible we read about people who do right things and people who do wrong things. We also read rules about what is right and what is wrong.

God tells us about these people and gives us these rules because He loves us and knows what is best for us. When we do right things and obey God's rules, life is happier. But when we do wrong things and we break God's rules, life is not happy.

Because God gave us the Bible, we don't have to guess about what is right and what is wrong.

Dear Jesus, help me to read the Bible so I know right from wrong!

The Bible shows me how to live the right way.

The Good Shepherd

"You, my sheep, are the sheep of my pasture. You are my people and I am your God."
—EZEKIEL 34:31

Have you ever seen sheep—or cows or horses—in a meadow? They belong to a farmer who takes care of them. He makes sure they have food and water. He helps the sheep become healthy when they are sick, and He makes sure they aren't in danger.

The Bible says that Jesus is like a Shepherd and we are like His sheep. That means that Jesus makes sure that we have all we need and He cares for us. What a blessing that Jesus—who called Himself "the Good Shepherd"—is taking care of us!

Dear Jesus, thank You for being my Good Shepherd and taking care of me.

Jesus is my Good Shepherd!

Jesus, the Superhero

God, you are strong. Lord, you are loving.
—PSALM 62:11–12

Josiah loves to talk about how strong superheroes are. He says that the Hulk is big and strong, but Captain America is really strong too.

Then he always asks his father, "Dad, do you know who the strongest superhero of them all is?"

Dad shakes his head, and then Josiah tells him that Jesus is the strongest of them all. He is a real-life superhero who saved the whole world because He loved people so much. "Dad," he says, "that's why Jesus is the strongest superhero of them all."

Josiah is absolutely right!

Dear God, I am glad I know You are the strongest superhero ever.

God is all powerful *and* all loving.

Pastor Greg Pulling, Journey Christian Fellowship, New Kent, VA

Be a Kid!

Young people, enjoy yourselves while you are
young. Be happy while you are young.
　　　　　　　　　—ECCLESIASTES 11:9

I f you are four years old, there is a lot to like about being four. If you are eight years old, you can find neat things about being eight. At every age there's something special, so enjoy every age!

The Bible says that too: "Enjoy yourselves while you are young." What do you like about being the age you are right now? If you like swimming, swim! And thank God that you are healthy enough to swim. If you like digging in the sand at the playground, go dig as often as you can.

Be happy being you!

Dear God, thank You for giving me lots of reasons to be happy.

I want to have
fun while
I'm a kid!

Under the Water

God said, "Let the water be filled with living things."
—GENESIS 1:20

Huge whales eat something called *plankton* that we can't see without a microscope. Coral and shells are scattered across the bottom of the ocean. Dolphins and otters play—and sharks look for dinner!

God created everything—and that is a lot of things! Think about all the different kinds of fish He made. Think about how big some of these fish and whales and sharks are—and how small some of the crabs and fish and shells are.

God created incredible living things all around us—and God created you.

Dear Lord, thank You for the plants and animals that live underwater. You are amazing!

God created the ocean!

Better Than . . .

I will be content as if I had eaten the best foods.
My lips will sing. My mouth will praise you.
—PSALM 63:5

There's nothing better than _____, hamburgers, ice cream, watermelon, tacos, corn on the cob, pizza, and more. You fill in the blank!

We all have a favorite food that makes our taste buds and our tummies happy. And have you noticed that eating this special treat can also make your heart feel happy and content?

While we may be very happy and content after eating our favorite food, knowing and loving God will make us even happier. When our hearts are overflowing with happiness because of God, let's be sure to praise Him!

Dear Lord, nothing can make me happier than knowing You. I love You!

Nothing is better than God.

The Law Family,
First Baptist Church Woodstock, Woodstock, GA

Jump for Joy

The Lord is great. He is worthy of our praise.
—Psalm 145:3

Have you ever earned a star in school, surprised your mom by cleaning your bedroom without her asking, or scored the winning soccer goal? If you have, then you know how great it feels to hear others praise you and say, "Good job!"

God created us to praise Him—and our great, powerful, loving God deserves all our praise. In the Bible, the word *praise* sometimes means to "jump for joy." God is so good to us that we should jump up and down with joy.

God *is* "worthy of our praise."

Dear God, You are awesome! Help me jump for joy every day and praise You.

I will jump for joy and praise God!

The Law Family,
First Baptist Church Woodstock, Woodstock, GA

Has God Ever Been Late?

God certainly does everything at just the right time.
—ECCLESIASTES 3:11

I t's not always easy to be on time—but we have lots of chances to try! We have church and school. We have doctor appointments and dentist appointments. We have playdates with friends. All of us have been late to some things.

But did you know that God has never been late to do anything? You may pray for something and want God to answer you right away. God *could* answer right away, but He might not. Whenever He does answer, He will always be right on time. His timing for answering your prayers is perfect.

Dear God, thank You for always being right on time when You answer my prayers.

God answers my prayers right on time.

God Is So Good

Lord our God, you have done many miracles.
Your plans for us are many.

—PSALM 40:5 CEV

D o you ever spend time thinking about how good God is to you? That is a very good thing for every one of us—every kid and mom and dad—to do every day.

God has "done many miracles." He created you! And He created all the animals as well as the sun, the moon, and every star in the sky. He let His Son, Jesus, die on the cross so He could forgive your sins. God loves you. And He has amazing things planned for you as you live with God as your King.

Dear God, thank You for being so good to me! I know You have good plans for my future.

God is my King because He is so good!

Making Jesus Happy

Pride leads to arguments. But those who take advice are wise.

—PROVERBS 13:10

D id you know the Bible teaches us how to live? In its pages, Jesus tells us how to live a life that will make Him happy.

Jesus also tells us what makes Him unhappy, and one of those things is pride. Pride is when we think we are better than other people—and we act that way. When we are full of pride, we don't share, we aren't kind, and we tend to argue.

You can make God happy by not being proud— and by getting good advice from people who love Him and love you.

Jesus, I want to make You happy by not being prideful and by following good advice.

> Jesus, I don't want to be prideful.

The Law Family,
First Baptist Church Woodstock, Woodstock, GA

God's Protection

*A person who respects the Lord will have
security. And his children will be protected.*
—Proverbs 14:26

Security may be a new word for you. *Security* is when you are safe from bad people and things; *security* is also when you are not worried about anything bad happening.

The promise today is that because we love the Lord, we can know that He will keep us safe. We can know that we don't have to worry about anything because God takes care of us.

But sometimes you may feel alone or sad. Even though you know God, you might even worry. At times like that, pray! God wants you to know His peace.

Dear God, thank You that I can have security, safety, and peace because You love me.

I don't need to worry because God loves me.

Dr. Ken Duggan, Dallas Bay Church, Hixson, TN

Our Amazing God

I will praise you as long as I live. I will lift up my hands in prayer to your name.

—Psalm 63:4

Think about a time you were excited about something really great happening. Maybe you met a new friend or received an unexpected gift.

Those excited, happy feelings are a lot like how God feels when you praise Him and tell Him how good and amazing He is. If you start praising God every day right now, praising Him will be a great habit for the rest of your life.

So let's praise God. Thank Him for your family, your home, and your friends. He will be happy you did.

God, I praise You for filling my life with good things, special people, and Your love.

I will praise God.

Choose Your Words Well

What you say affects how you live. You will be rewarded by how you speak.

—Proverbs 18:20

Words are powerful, and their power can be used for good—to make people happy—or for bad—to make people sad.

God likes us to use words for good. He likes to hear us speak nicely to our friends and family. All of us like people who say kind things, not mean or untrue things. Even God likes it when we pray to Him and tell Him about all the things we are thankful for.

So be careful when you speak. And if you have nothing nice to say, say nothing at all.

God, help me think before I speak and be quiet if I have nothing good to say.

I will be careful with what I say.

Say Something Nice Today

A wise person . . . wins people to his side with pleasant words.

—Proverbs 16:21

I t happens to all of us: someone says something that hurts us and makes us sad. Even though we know how bad that feels, sometimes we say things that hurt people, don't we?

Words don't have to hurt people. Words can also help people feel happy, and that's a better way for us to use our words. When we say something nice, we can make a person who is having a bad day feel better. Ask God to help you have "pleasant words" to say to people today.

To whom will you say something nice today?

Dear God, Your words are good. Help my words today to be kind.

I will be wise and use pleasant words.

Dr. Ken Duggan, Dallas Bay Church, Hixson, TN

Be Nice Even When Others Are Not

A wise person is patient. He will be honored if he ignores a wrong done against him.

—PROVERBS 19:11

H as anyone ever pushed you down on the playground? Has someone ever taken away what you were playing with? If something like this has happened to you, of course you felt sad or even mad at that person.

But God tells us what a wise response is: we should never be mean to people just because they were not nice to us.

So here's what to do: Take a deep breath. Count to five. Ask God to help you not be mean. And then smile. God will be pleased that you were nice.

God, help me be kind even when someone has been mean to me.

God can help me be nice.

Dr. Ken Duggan, Dallas Bay Church, Hixson, TN

Living God's Way

Train a child how to live the right way. Then even
when he is old, he will still live that way.
—PROVERBS 22:6

Did you know that lessons and truths you learn now will help you be a better grown-up someday?

When you are at Sunday school, church, or home, you are learning the right way to live. The right way to live is God's way, and learning God's way now will help you for the rest of your life.

God has given us the Bible to teach us how to live in a way that makes Him happy. So ask God to help you do what the Bible says to do because His way is the right way to live.

God, thank You that I can learn the right way to live.

I want to live
God's way.

Contributors

316

Scripture Index